The University of Groningen

An Unofficial History

Edited by John Flood

Department of English Language & Culture
University of Groningen
2018

In memoriam
Dr Anne Bollmann
(1963-2018)

Third impression

© John Flood, 2018

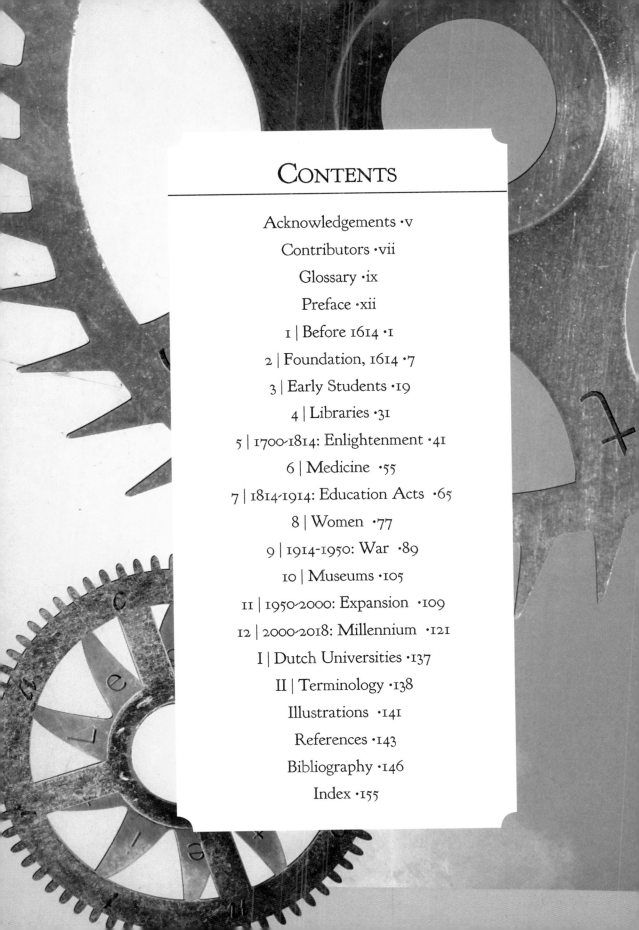

CONTENTS

ACKNOWLEDGEMENTS

We would like to thank several people who were of enormous assistance with this book: Lydia ten Brummelhuis, Dr Kees Dekker, Dr Henk Dragstra, Dr Ann Hoag, Dr At Hof, Esther Hoorn LLM, Anneke Kok, Prof. Alasdair MacDonald, Rolf ter Sluis, Dr Irene Visser, and Cato van der Vlugt.

Permission to reproduce copyrighted material was generously granted by the following or their estates (see References for more details):

Dr David M. Baneke, Freudenthal Instituut, University of Utrecht
Prof. Klaas van Berkel, Department of History, University of Groningen
Dr Lies Ast-Boiten
Dr Pieter Caljé, Department of History, Maastricht University
M. Gerritsen
Dr Barbara Henkes, Department of History, University of Groningen
Prof. Jos Hermans, Department of History, University of Groningen
Gerda Huisman, University Library, Groningen
J. Kingma, University of Groningen
Koninklijke Brill NV
Koninklijke Van Gorcum BV
Wim Koops, University Library, Groningen
Prof. Jan van der Korst, Faculty of Medical Science, University of Groningen
Hans Kuné, University of Groningen
Dr Zweder von Martels, Department of Classics, University of Groningen
Dr Martin van Meurs
The Rijksmuseum, Amsterdam
Franck Smit, University of Groningen
Springer Science + Business Media
B.P. & H. Tammeling
Taylor & Francis Ltd.
Guus Termeer, Office of the University, Groningen
University Museum, Groningen
Uitgeverij Verloren
Dr Inge de Wilde
Prof. Frans Zwarts, quondam *rector magnificus*, University of Groningen.

These people's works have been translated, abbreviated and adapted. None of the opinions expressed in this book should be identified with those of the authors listed above (whose work should be consulted in its original form).

Every effort has been made to trace copyright holders and to obtain their permission for the use of copyrighted material. If proper acknowledgement has not been made, copyright holders are invited to contact the editor.

CONTRIBUTORS

Eltje Beckmann, MA

Siebrand Boerema, MA

Judith Bol, MA

Frank Braamhaar, MA

Tina Bruinsma, MA, MEd

Elien Cusveller, MA, MA

Ingrid Dillen, MA, MA

John Flood, MPhil, PhD

Violette Frentrop, MA

Sara van Geloven, MA

Sabrina Hartmann, MA

Tamsin Horsfield, MA

Emma Jansen, MA

Hans Jansen, PhD

Miriam Lange, MA

Maria van Loosdrecht, MA, MA

Daniël Muller, MA, MA

Jill Nobel, MA

Sander Ootjers, MA

Dorrit Ris, MA, MA

Jelmer van der Schaaf, BA

Dorian Smilda, MA

Aaf Tienkamp, MA

Esmee Tijdeman, MA

Emmie Touwen, MA, MA

Rudy Veiga da Palma, BA

Miranda Wijgers, MA

Baukje Wijma, MA

◄ *Senate Room*

Academic Senate: governing body of the university until 1971. The chairman was the rector and all professors were automatically members. It was replaced by the University Council.

Academy Building: main ceremonial building of the university. It is located in the city centre

Aula: principal ceremony hall in the Academy Building.

beadle: officer of the university who, amongst other things, led academic processions. The office was abolished in the 1977. The ceremonial role is now taken by a university porter.

Boteringestraat: now Oude Boteringestraat, a city-centre street including the Faculty of Theology and Religious Studies and the office of the University Board.

curator: member of the governing body.

doctoraalexamen: now abolished, passing this exam granted the status of *doctorandus*.

doctorandus: equivalent of a master's degree (MA, MSc).

drs.: abbreviation of *doctorandus* used before a holder's name in Dutch, e.g. drs. A. Vaatstra.

Forum Academicum: the university court (1614–1811).

Friesland: a coastal province west of Groningen.

Grote Markt: 'Large Market', the central square of Groningen.

guilder: Dutch currency replaced by the euro in 2002.

gymnasium: secondary school preparing students for university education. The syllabus includes Latin and/or Greek.

Hanzehogeschool: The Hanze University of Applied Sciences, Groningen. A higher-level institution for the applied sciences. It also houses the academies of fine art and dance as well as the Prince Claus Conservatoire.

hogere burgerschool **(HBS):** form of secondary education (1863–1986) that focussed on teaching mathematics, science and modern languages.

Hortus or **Old Hortus:** Area north of the city centre between Grote Rozenstraat and Grote Kruisstraat (behind the Department of Psychology).

kandidaatsexamen: formerly, passing this exam granted the title of *kandidaat* (comparable to a primary degree, e.g. a BA).

kerk: church.

lustrum: celebration held every five years.

Martinikerk: St Martin's Church on the Grote Markt in the city centre.

Ommelanden: the province of Groningen excluding the city.

Paddepoel: district in the north-west of the city. The location of the Zernike Campus.

promotie: ceremony in which a doctorate is conferred.

propaedeuse **(propadeutic phase):** first year of a study programme.

rector magnificus: until 1971, head of the university. Now chairs several administrative bodies.

RUG: University of Groningen.

stadtholder: title of the princes of Orange.

UK or *Universiteitskrant:* Groningen's university newspaper.

Universitair Medisch Centrum Groningen **(UMCG):** University Medical Centre Groningen, the university's hospital.

Vindicat or *Vindicat atque polit:* (Latin: maintain and civilise), the oldest student society in Groningen.

Zernike Campus or **Zernike Complex:** main science campus located north-west of the city centre.

PREFACE

THIS work has much in common with one by Jane Austen who, aged fifteen, produced *The History of England from the Reign of Henry IV to the Death of Charles I. By a Partial, Prejudiced and Ignorant Historian*. Let us begin with ignorant: this is not principally a work of original research; instead it is firmly based in the writing of others (who were not ignorant) and in places translates, abridges or paraphrases material which was written in Dutch or Latin and which is thus inaccessible to many English-speaking readers. The sources that are used are indicated in the acknowledgements and the references. The Bibliography provides further reading for those who can read Dutch. Of the many good books listed there, Klaas van Berkel's official history of the university, *Universiteit van het Noorden* (2014, 2017) is of note for its comprehensiveness, its clarity and the attractive manner in which it is presented.

This history is 'partial' and 'prejudiced' in that to keep it at its current length, many important things that might have been remarked were left unsaid. Instead, the contributors chose from the full span of the university's history incidents and people that interested them. It was felt that certain highlights could not be omitted, but that left a lot of choice, and some readers will doubtless regret that more time was not given to a topic that they are interested in. With the university's expansion in the twentieth century it became increasingly difficult even to gesture at being comprehensive. As Groningen is now, its range of people, courses and research is such that were the whole book given over to its history since 2000 its space would be inadequate. One can work in the university for a decade without knowing more than the smallest fraction of what is going on in it. Fortunately, in most cases, the recent happenings in individual institutes or departments can be found online.

This book does not deal at any length with the various restructurings of courses and faculties that went on down through the years. Certainly, the landmark moments, such as the

university legislation of the nineteenth century or the Bologna Declaration are explained, but this history is more old-fashioned and like Austen's it focuses on important people and more tangible events.

In defence of this endeavour it should be said that having draw on good sources, its basis is a solid one. It provides an overview that stretches from the foundation of the Academy of Groningen in 1614 to today in a manner which does not presuppose much knowledge of Dutch history. It also provides information about important buildings or works of art that visitors to the campus are likely to see.

Although produced by members of the university and benefiting from the co-operation of people and institutions attached to it, this is not an official history of Groningen. For the most part, it is a positive one, but there is room for some criticism too. Austen's partiality appears in its opinions of developments or judgements on specific events. These can usually be spotted, and their wisdom mentally put aside without too much trouble.

Are there lessons to be learnt from the history of the university? Certainly, there were individual people or events that might inspire or caution readers. However, for this to happen, one's focus must be narrowed and often much of the detail that separates now and then blurred away. For example, it is true that from its foundation the university attracted many international students and that it funded a considerable number of them who were refugees and that this might offer a positive precedent today. However, while national borders were not important in Groningen at the time, religious ones were (which was the case in very many early modern European universities), and it was only students and staff of a particular kind of Christianity who were unhesitatingly welcomed.

One feature which is constant throughout four centuries is change. The institution was continuously reformed, sometimes gradually as new intellectual trends diffused themselves throughout a faculty, and sometimes suddenly when national politics or legislation turned things upside down. Another feature is external government, first from the city and province of Groningen and later from The Hague. Questions that were raised repeatedly included what a university is for and the nature of the relationship between the institution and society.

Readers may well meditate on these perennial questions, but this book also serves the merely curious who wish to know why a building bears its name, who is commemorated by a statue, how the hospital became so large or what is in the University Museum.

A Note on Names

Dutch parents can be very generous with the number of first names that they give to their children. It is not unusual to have three or four names which appear as initials in official listings. Nor it is unusual to have names in Latin, although they are rendered in a more vernacular style in everyday use. A typical Dutch person might therefore be J.P.M. Jansen, from which you cannot tell whether Jansen is male, female or transgender. In this book, the initials are expanded (thus Johannes Paulus Maria Jansen) even though this is a mouthful. Where a person's everyday name is known it is also given (in our example, Johannes might be shortened to Hans).

CHAPTER ONE

BEFORE 1614

GRONINGEN is situated in land that had been populated by the Frisians since before Roman times. It has English linguistic links in that Frisian is the Germanic language closest to English: Frisians may have come to Britain with the invading Angles and Saxons and the people of Friesland certainly traded with their neighbour in the middle ages. Missionaries such as the Irish-trained Willibrord (658–739) and the unfortunate St Boniface (c.675–754; he was murdered near Dokkum, north-west of Groningen), sought to bring Christianity to the region, a task that was only accomplished by the conquest of Charlemagne (747–814). While Carolingian rule was not always more than nominal, Christianity took root. This was visible in the geography, with its ecclesiastical buildings and with the land reclamation that went on under the auspices of the Cistercians who established themselves in the north in the twelfth century.

Settlement of the area that is now the centre of the city of Groningen goes back at least to the ninth century when there was a church on the site of the current Martinikerk. In the eleventh century, Groningen was granted to the bishop of Utrecht by Emperor Henry III. At the end of the thirteenth century, like many other cities in the Low Countries, it joined the Hanseatic League. This allowed it to exploit its position on the River Aa and connected it to a trading route that stretched from London to Cologne and Novgorod. The League died out in the sixteenth century, but the link between its cities was revived in modern times and is marked in Groningen in, for example, the name of the *Hanzehogeschool* (Hanze University of Applied Sciences).

SPAIN & REVOLT

Building on the rights acquired by his father, Maximilian I, when he married Mary of Burgundy, Charles V successfully added the Low Countries, including Groningen (in 1536), to the Habsburg empire. Resistance to this frequently had religious motivations as the Catholic Habsburgs were at odds with their Protestant subjects throughout the sixteenth century. To reassert control, Phillip II of Spain sent Fernando Álvarez de Toledo, duke of Alba to subdue unrest. During Alba's governor-generalship (1567–73) more than a thousand people of all classes were executed and an abortive plan for new taxation mooted. These unpopular decisions played a part in sparking the Dutch Revolt of 1567 which was led by William the Silent, prince of Orange (1533–84) the first stadtholder of

◄ *Ceiling of the Martinikerk*

the United Provinces of the Netherlands (the Dutch Republic). After the assassination of William the Silent, governor-generalship of this new near-unity was offered to Henry III of France, Elizabeth I of England, and finally, the monarchs having refused, to Robert Dudley, earl of Leicester, who briefly commanded an army in the Netherlands before returning home.

At the outset of the revolt, the city (but not the province) of Groningen remained essentially Catholic and pro-Spanish. In the vicinity of Groningen in July 1567, Prince William's brother, Louis of Nassau, took the field against Alba. The duke's army of 15,000 was somewhat larger than that of his opponent, but what counted in the end is that a good-old-fashioned Dutch plan to open the dykes failed and the Spanish army massacred thousands driving them into the River Ems near Jemmingen (now Jemgum in Germany). Alba's army narrowly missed capturing Count Louis before pillaging its way back to Groningen (despite the fury of their commander at their indiscipline).

In 1594, Groningen, an isolated Spanish bastion, was besieged by an army of the United Provinces which included an English company under the command of Sir Francis Vere. After two months, 700 deaths, and 10,000 cannon balls, the city capitulated and its Catholic clerics were exiled with the Spanish soldiers who were allowed to march south. The victory of 1594 is known as the Reduction (*reductio*) from the Spanish yoke. The city and province of Groningen, uneasy bedfellows, were administratively joined to become the seventh province of the Republic. In internal decisions they had one vote each, an equality that frequently led to paralysis. The Twelve Years' Truce of 1609 temporarily ended the war with Spain and gave the hybrid Groningen space to decide to do new things. In 1612 the possibility of establishing an academy was raised. In the words of its founding document, *The Eternal Edict*, war had made room for the arts of peace.

THE ADUARD CIRCLE

THE province of Groningen had a tradition of scholarship before the foundation of the university. The circle of Aduard, located in the Cistercian monastery of St Bernard 8km north of Groningen, enjoyed international recognition, and the city's Latin school, the St Martin School, had an enviable reputation.

In the fifteenth century, several scholars of European stature were linked to the monastery of Aduard (which has sometimes incorrectly been called an academy). Rudolf Agricola and Wessel Gansfort, although neither of them Cistercians, were among the prominent names associated with it. Their reputations live on in Groningen through, for instance, Wessel Gansfort College and the university's Agricola research seminar. Other members of the Aduard circle included its monks (most notably the abbot, Hendrik van Rees) and its visitors. These latter came to become better scholars and stayed for weeks and sometimes even months to participate in and learn from the lively discussions held there.

Gansfort: God is My Father and My Mother

Wessel Gansfort (1419–89), was born in Groningen, probably in 1419. After studies in Zwolle (where he met and struck up a friendship with Thomas à Kempis), and Cologne (where he received his MA in 1452), he travelled through Europe. Gansfort read everything that could increase his knowledge: he learned some Greek, and the rudiments of Hebrew, Aramaic and Arabic. At Heidelberg he taught the humanities. Having been at Leuven for a while he set off for Paris where he resided for several years. He was at Rome in 1470 living in the household of Francesco della Rovere (later Pope Sixtus IV). Subsequently, he went to Florence, Venice and Paris.

Gansfort regarded Aristotle as a master of logic but one deficient in theology. He believed that had the august St Thomas Aquinas (who forged the orthodox synthesis of Aristotelianism and scholastic Christianity) known more Greek or Hebrew that Aquinas would have understood this. As Aquinas had an exalted (but by no means unchallenged) position, this shows some of Gansfort's independence of thought. In a similar manner, Gansfort read Cicero and Virgil intently but was opposed to what he regarded as the speciousness of some classical eloquence. From his reading of Hebrew, he concluded that it was correct to call God a loving mother and father and to refer to Jesus as a brother and sister. On returning to the Low Countries, he became personal physician to David of Burgundy, bishop of Utrecht, whose protection he needed from the Inquisition.

Gansfort spent the years between 1477 and his death mostly in Aduard and in the Olde [*sic*] Convent in Groningen (an order of tertiaries) where he enjoyed the ongoing protection of David of Burgundy. At Aduard, he ate with the monks, and they listened when, for example, he dismissed one Cistercian classic as 'nonsense polished up with monastic labour'. He died on 4 October 1489 and was buried in the Olde Convent's church. His remains were transferred to the Martinikerk in 1862 where he now has a prominent monument. Walter, abbot of Aduard gave annuities to the convent in return for prayers for him.

Gansfort did not enjoy posthumous fame before the 1520s when his works were published at Zwolle. These attracted the attention of readers such as Luther who agreed with Gansfort's questioning of indulgences, remissions for spiritual punishment that were often sold by the Catholic church. A printed edition of Gansfort's works was presented to the Academy of Groningen at its foundation. Posthumously, he was claimed as a reformer before the reformation: Luther observed, 'had I read [his works] earlier, my enemies would have thought Luther derived everything from Wessel, so much is it that we think alike'. An admiring early life of Gansfort states that:

In Groningen, he was the first to shine light upon the gospel in times of barbarism. His aversion to false worship and his effort to find the truth made people believe that he was sent by God to dispel the darkness of heresy and superstition. He believed in Christ and in a devout life but not in the masks of priests, nor in false prayers.

Like most claims of the existence of reformers before the reformation, this involves some anachronistic retrospective reading as, although Gansfort was not an orthodox Catholic, he would not have passed for an orthodox member of any of the branches of the magisterial Reformation.

The Groningen Gansfort family included another celebrated heterodox writer. After a branch emigrated to America, one General Peter Gansevoort became the grandfather of Herman Melville, the author of *Moby Dick* (1851).

Agricola: The Republic of Learning

Roelof Huesman (Rudolphus Agricola's vernacular name; 1444–85), of Baflo, a village north of Groningen, was another of the scholars connected to the monastery of Aduard (between c.1479–84). Agricola was the son a of a Benedictine priest and Zycka Huesman. He studied for his BA at Erfurt and his MA at Cologne and Louvain (1465). Shortly afterwards he went to Italy and stayed at Pavia for several years. He returned home in 1471 and after three years he went to serve as an organist at the court in Ferrara. In Dillingen in Germany he published *De inventione dialecta*, on the role of logic in rhetoric which became a well-known work after he died. It is said that he always travelled with only one servant but many books. Philip Melanchthon, the famous Lutheran, recalled that he 'was consulted by professors from all disciplines' while Erasmus described him as 'a man who deserves immortal glory'.

Quitting Italy for Groningen, he became municipal secretary and ambassador and he interacted with the Aduard circle. He finally settled down between Heidelberg and Worms thanks to his friendship with Johan von Dalberg, bishop of Worms. In Heidelberg he lectured and began his study of Hebrew so that he could more fully understand the Bible. He went with Dalberg to Rome where the bishop delivered one of Agricola's orations before Innocent VIII, but on the return journey he scholar fell sick of the illness that finally killed him in Heidelberg on 28 October 1485. He was buried in a Franciscan habit. There is a 1940 carving of him by Willem Valk on the west side of the Martinikerk's tower: it shows him carrying an organ in memory of his musical talent (the nearby figures on the tower are St Martin of Tours and Bernlef, a Frisian bard).

In a letter of 1484 addressed to the famous Hebraist, Johannes Reuchlin, Agricola explained his life in a manner that would be endorsed by many other scholars then and since:

I have wanted to be helpful in any way I could to the Republic of Learning of my home country. Had this not been my objective I might have travelled the same road that everybody does, a road which leads to greater wealth, to a more exalted reputation, and to a more favourable reception among the people.

The same year he wrote a letter to man who asked to come and study under him. It circulated afterwards as a tract on education. In it, he suggests what a student must do: 'he has to clearly and unambiguously grasp what he is learning, firmly retain what he has grasped, then have the ability to also create and produce from that something of his own'.

Praedinius: Teacher

Regnerus Praedinius (1510–59) was born in Winsum, a town not far from Groningen. He chose his last name, Praedinius, because he was born in the countryside (*praedinius* means 'man of the field' - humanists often created Latin names for themselves). He was educated by friars and soon went to Leuven where he first studied philosophy and then theology. After a spell as a teacher in Groningen, he travelled for a decade. In 1545 he returned to Groningen for good and he was offered several jobs. He became the headmaster of the Latin school, a role he believed would benefit the community and fit him best.

Praedinius had an aptitude for science, was very eloquent and, most importantly, was a good educator, therefore many pupils frequented his school. He taught languages but also medicine and law. Apart from teaching four hours a day, he spent his time in study, writing about, amongst others, Plato, Aristotle, and Cicero. However, he finally concluded that this had not been worthwhile as these writers had little to do with the Bible, so he burnt his work. He spared his religious writings because he believed that these could show people the way to eternal life. After an illness of some months, Praedinius died on 18 April 1559.

ACADEMY OF FRANEKER, 1585–1811

Groningen was not the first institution of higher learning in the north of the Netherlands. The *Academiae Franekerensis* was established in Franeker in Friesland in 1585. At a time when Groningen was in Spanish hands, Franeker provided a Calvinist education for young men from Friesland who could not afford to travel to the University of Leiden. Franeker had faculties of Arts, Philosophy, Theology, Law and Medicine. Despite the moral emphasis of its Calvinist foundation, its students were known for riotous living. Although it began with local needs in mind, in the period 1625–50 half of the academy's students were international (mainly German). The most famous international student was Descartes who studied there briefly. In the eighteenth century the academy's reputation declined until, having educated 15,000 men, it was abolished by Napoleon in 1811. Franeker's association with a university has revived via the University of Groningen as its PhD students of Frisian origin can now have their graduation ceremonies in its medieval St Martin's Church.

CHAPTER TWO

FOUNDATION, 1614

I N 1595 Mello Brunsema (1580–c.1611), a Leiden alumnus and formerly a teacher at the University of Helmstedt in Lower Saxony, was granted permission by the city and Ommelanden to establish a college in Groningen to teach introductory law courses on the Emperor Justinian's *Institutes*. This was not a success and was wound up by 1601.

GRONINGEN, 1614

In November 1612, the city council decided to establish an academy. The idea was that students should have their own college with several faculties and that founding this would reduce the cost of their travelling elsewhere. The councillors of the city and the Ommelanden–who were all in agreement, a rare occasion–were willing to pay. In return they wanted the new academy to educate Calvinist clergy and prepare lawyers who could fulfil public functions.

The first *rector magnificus* appointed was Ubbo Emmius, a leading figure amongst the Calvinists of East Friesland who had been head of the St Martin school until then. The rector was the president of the Academic Senate which consisted of all regular professors. This senate shaped education at the academy, from the organisation of courses to exams and public ceremonies. The administrative matters and public affairs were in the care of the beadle or the registrar. To attract students, it was decided to appoint professors who were famous beyond the Dutch Republic. Ubbo Emmius was such a one. The first five academics hired with Emmius, were 'devout, learned and renowned men'. They were enticed by a high salary (over 800 florins a year), subsidised rent, insurance and other privileges.

The *Hoogeschool van Stad en Lande* (Academy of the City and Province of Groningen) opened on 23 August 1614 and was modelled after existing institutions at Leiden and Franeker. Groningen had four faculties. Students were educated in humanities (called the Faculty of Philosophy) before proceeding to one of the higher faculties, Medicine, Law or Theology. The foundation of the academy was connected to the constitutional structure of the Republic. Each region was sovereign and had its own obligations to education. To the province of Groningen, having its own academy meant having the power to control. A board of four curators carried out its daily supervision, while important decisions, such as appointing professors, were a regional matter.

The official opening of the academy took place on 23 August 1614. The celebrations lasted three days. They began with an address in the Martinikerk. Rev. Arnoldus Martini of Uithuizen gave the opening speech and blessed the new institute. When the professors tried to leave the church afterwards there were so many people outside that they could hardly exit. They made a stop at Prof. Nicolaas Mulerius' house and half an hour later commenced a stately procession to the Academy Building. This was followed by a banquet which lasted until the early hours. The next day, Prof. Johan Epinus Huninga gave a lecture and thanked God, the founders of the academy and the representatives of the city council. On the last day, another crowd gathered in the theology lecture

───────────────────────────

◄ *Ubbo Emmius (eighteenth-century copy of 1614 original)*

hall. There, Prof. William MacDowell delivered a graceful speech on philosophy. After all these festivities, they finally began with the actual job of education.

BUILDINGS

Although financial resources were scarce, accommodation for the new institution was easily found. The Lady Sywen and the Lady Menolda convents in the city centre had been confiscated for public use in 1594 after the Reduction of Groningen. The academy was housed in the Lady Sywen Convent which was rebuilt for that purpose. The design, by the city's architect, Garwen Peters, was characterised by simplicity and sobriety. The building's modest presentation reflected the goal of the academy: to educate preachers and reliable civil servants. There was no place for external trappings.

The Lady Menolda Convent, west of the Lady Sywen Convent, was rebuilt as professors' accommodation. The Burse was housed in a building between the Academy Building and the Boteringestraat. Here students who were not well off could get subsidised meals twice a day. South of the Academy Building was the Franciscan monastery. Its church was remodelled as the Academy Church. This was the location for the academy's ceremonies, conferrals and sermons. The sacristy was later rebuilt as an anatomical theatre.

Although it was a private rather than an academy initiative, the founding of the Old Hortus should be mentioned. On a small plot north of the city centre (which is now between Grote Rozenstraat and Grote Kruisstraat and behind the Department of Psychology), Henricus Munting, a pharmacist, established a botanic garden in the seventeenth century. This eventually passed into the care of the university which outgrew the available space in the early twentieth century with the result that a more extensive twenty hectare site, the Hortus Botanicus was established in Haren, south of the city. In the 1980s the university stopped using this site in its research work and the gardens became a public amenity.

UBBO EMMIUS: FIRST RECTOR MAGNIFICUS

The first rector, Ubbo Emmius was born in the village of Greetsiel in Friesland on 5 December 1547. His father was Emmo Dijken, a learned, devout theologian. Emmius's talent was obvious from an early age. At the age of twenty-three, after fourteen years of schooling, his father deemed him ready for higher education. Thus, in 1570, he went to the renowned University of Rostock in Germany. All went well, but in Rostock Emmius got scurvy, a disease that was endemic along the Baltic Coast at the time. However, he regained his health. On learning of the death of his father, he returned home. Then, there was a family tragedy as his only sister drowned so he spent somewhat more than two years with his mother and four brothers, before leaving for two years' French study in Geneva. He also looked forward to attending other lectures from celebrated professors in the university founded by Calvin. After visiting Lyon and Basel, two other centres of Calvinism, he returned to his family.

In 1579 Emmius accepted the position of rector of the school in Norden. He became engaged to Theda Tjabbersdochter and they married in 1581. Soon, Theda gave birth to a son, Emmo, but she died during an epidemic. Two years later, Emmius married again; this time he chose a nineteen-year-old girl called Margaretha van Bergen. His work in Norden ended when an investigation by Lutherans forced him to resign in September 1587. He was then invited to become the head of the Latin school in Leer,

A: Academy Building. B: Church. C: Library. D: Latin School. E: Burse. F: Professors' Houses ▶

a town in the region of his birth. His presence there made the school flourish and it became one of the best known in the region. In 1594 he was asked to come to Groningen to breathe new life into the old St Martin School. He was to choose new teachers and take care of the humanities. Staff and students were attracted to his school and for twenty years Emmius remained at his post. He was offered many other jobs with higher salaries, but he chose to stay in Groningen.

Emmius had learned friends with whom he corresponded. One of them was Prince Willem Lodewijk, count of Nassau-Dillenburg and stadtholder of Groningen. Emmius also published many works with history as his specialty. His knowledge was such that it was asserted that whenever someone asked him anything about the history of any nation in any period that he knew about it. With all this learning he decided to write the history of Friesland. Another work was his *Chronologicum*, which belonged to a genre invented by Emmius himself. In it he compared the histories of different nations that used different calendars. He also published a biography of Willem Lodewijk. Even though by this time his health was not good—Emmius was housebound for at least four years—he continued to work. In 1625, when a book about the history of the Ancient Greece was being published, his youngest son Egbert died in Orléans aged only twenty-five. Emmius could not recover from this loss and he became ill himself. He became too weak to climb the stairs to his study and for more than a month he remained near his fireplace. He could not sleep due to a tightness in his chest. During the last two days of his life, Emmius, aged seventy-eight, longed to leave the earth behind. On the night of 4–5 December 1625 the first rector of Groningen died. His funeral was held on 13 December and his body was buried in the Academy's chapel.

Foundation Professors

The new academy had five professors in addition to Ubbo Emmius. Of these, one was German and one Scottish. Nationality was not a concern: what was important was religious orthodoxy. Several of these men went on to have careers outside academia.

Johannes Epinus Huninga: Politician

Huninga (1583–1639) was born in Oostwold in the province of Groningen and studied at Ubbo Emmius's Latin school. He held the chair of philosophy and was an extraordinary professor of law. He left these as he became increasingly involved with politics, becoming a city councillor and later mayor of Groningen.

William Macdowell: Royal Representative

Macdowell (1590–BEF. 1666), was born in Makerstouwn in Scotland in 1590. For his higher education he went to the University of St Andrews. In four years he completed his study and in 1614 he was offered the chair of philosophy at Groningen. Although he taught philosophy, he studied jurisprudence as well and on 25 May 1625 he received his doctoral degree in law. Having taught at the academy for thirteen years, in 1627 Macdowell became the chairman of the provincial military council of Groningen. In 1650 he was appointed representative of King Charles II of England to The Hague as a result of which Oliver Cromwell had him banished by the States General. He married twice:

in 1617 to Bernardine van Fritema, daughter of the mayor of Groningen, and then to Elisabeth Alberada. Sometime before 1666, he died in debt, having financed work on behalf of Charles II without being reimbursed. His Groningen house, now a restaurant, can be found in the city centre where the Folkingestraat meets the Vismarkt (Fish Market).

Nicolaas Mulerius: Physician & Mathematician

Mulerius came from an old, wealthy Bruges family called Des Muliers. His father was the theologian Pierre des Muliers and his mother was Claudia le Vettre. Mulerius was born on 25 December 1564. As des Muliers was a Protestant in the time of the Inquisition when he would have been regarded a heretic, the family had to quit Bruges in a hurry, leaving behind their house and everything else they owned. They fled to a town called Menen, close to the French border, but there they were not safe either. Luckily, the family was warned of impending trouble and was able to escape. Des Muliers and three of his children, among whom was the two-year-old Nicolaas, hid in a nearby forest. His wife, however, who wanted to follow him, had been betrayed by a neighbour. She was carrying their youngest child when she was seized by an armed group of persecutors. She was jailed for a year, during which time she was tortured. Catholics tried to convert her, but she did not change her religion, not even when her baby was taken from her. She was sentenced to death in 1568.

When he judged it to be safe, Des Muliers returned to Bruges and Nicolaas was taught the basics of Latin. They moved to Calais and only returned in 1577 after the Pacification of Ghent was signed and the provinces of the Netherlands agreed to discuss religious toleration in a common assembly. However, the French civil wars resumed, and Des Muliers relocated to Leiden, where the young Nicolaas enrolled at the university. He first studied philology and philosophy and then theology. Because of heart problems that made him unfit for a more active life and because of his personal interests, he wanted to engage with more than just these subjects. He decided to study medicine and mathematics as well, and combined this with knowledge of Hebrew, Arabic, and history. Among his teachers was the famous Justus Lipsius. In 1589, Mulerius received his doctoral degree in medicine. That same year, he married Christina Six in Amsterdam. He then started a doctor's practice in Harlingen which was such a success that the inhabitants appointed him to be the first municipal doctor.

After a spell in Amsterdam, Mulerius accepted the position of doctor to the States of Groningen and the *Ommelanden*. In 1608, he became head of the grammar school in Leeuwarden. Six years later he was asked to become a professor at Groningen to teach medicine and either Greek or mathematics. He chose to combine medicine with mathematics and taught these subjects until his death. He wrote many works including lists of lunar and solar cycles in Friesland and books on astronomy. He also published an

The Eternal Edict

The founding document of the Academy of Groningen is called *The Eternal Edict*. It was drawn up for the States of Groningen by Ubbo Emmius. The edict was printed and distributed to the cities in the Dutch Republic, in Germany, and in major urban centres in neighbouring countries. Calling something 'eternal' might now argue a certain confidence or complacency, but eternal edicts were common titles at the time. Although in some places it reads like the early modern equivalent of the output of a PR company parts of it ring true and announce a purpose that must still resonate with members of the university. The edict's text runs as follows (with headings added):

Example of Alfonso the Wise

The words and deeds of the very best and wisest princes and governors of state make clear what great value they attach to studies of learning and to the erudition derived from it. Here, the Spanish Alfonso V, king of Aragon, Sicily, Sardinia and Naples [r. 1416–58] shines above all, just as he exceeds all monarchs of his age in wisdom (because of this, the epithet 'the wise' is attributed to him). When his most important duties allowed it, he devoted himself heart and soul to good learning and enjoyed conversation with erudite men. For that reason, he was outraged when he once heard that a king of Spain used to say that it did not befit a good and noble man to be learned or to have anything to do with books. Alfonso exclaimed that 'this was not the voice of a king but that of an ox'. Indeed, he very solemnly swore that as far as he was concerned, 'he would rather lose his kingdoms, of which he possessed many, than that he should be ignorant of that learning of which he had all too little'. In conversation with Aeneas Silvius [later Pope Pius II] he said that rulers without learning were not very dissimilar from donkeys with crowns. He used to assert that of all his counsellors he most approved of the dead ones, that is wisely-written books, 'for they answered his questions and furnished advice without fear, obligation or flattery'. At the same time, Alfonso was certainly not one to sit inert or lazy, content with leisure in the shade, but rather in both times of war and peace he was constantly busy with the most important affairs, and more than once he experienced both sides of fortune. In either good or bad luck he truly proved how wise, virtuous, constant and moderate his mind was by maintaining the same demeanour.

Necessity of Learning

And yet, even now it is common to find people who regard themselves as wise, applauding their own ignorance as they are trained in no form of learning. They shamelessly assert that the study of good learning is useless and that erudition is completely superfluous to the community either of the state or of the church, and that all who indulge in study are criminally wasting time and money. We, however, are of a different opinion and follow the very wise and very great Alfonso. For, just as there are two kinds of military service, we think that for its welfare the state should be equipped with the knowledge of both the arts of weapons and of learning; with the former, so as not to be overcome by the enemy, with the latter, so as not to succumb to ignorance and barbarity and thereby perish. In our view, good and prudent governors should neglect neither of these two things.

Structure of the Academy

Now, moreover, war has made room for peace, and our attention is given to the arts of peace. For that reason, already incited much earlier by the examples of others and in a demonstration that we really have our fatherland at heart, we have decided to develop further the studies of learning pertaining to the second kind of military service here amongst us. To this end we have decided to open in Groningen, the metropolis of this province, a famous school or academy. It is our wish that the subjects of the three faculties commonly designated as higher ones shall be publicly taught: theology, jurisprudence and medicine, alongside all parts of philosophy, logic, ethics, physics, history, mathematical disciplines, and Greek and Hebrew; in short, those subjects which are usually taught in other public schools or academies, together with exercises in corresponding disputations.

Provisions for Professors and Students

For instruction in these subjects and for chairing these disputations we shall, God willing, appoint a sufficient number of professors famous for their knowledge who are incited to the performance of their office by generous salaries and advertised benefits. In this, we shall do our utmost so that nothing established should be lacking in this respect. Moreover, for the common good, we shall grant rights and official privileges appropriate to teachers and students alike and we shall regulate all such matters conveniently and usefully. Finally, we shall solemnly so arrange things in respect of the expenses for those who settle here for the sake of education, that no-one will need to seek from us, either on the grounds of his rights or his merits, anything extra by way of this sort of benefit or generosity. Regarding these matters, we shall apply and use for much better purposes a large part of the funds which our ancestors – generous that they were in proportion to their prosperity and with intentions that may have been good and pious, but which were ensnared and fell through the darkness of their false beliefs – accumulated for monastic schools.

Attraction of Groningen

What incited and impelled us to take this decision, advantageous for both church and state, is not only, as we have shown, the ability to bear this expense, but also the unusual advantage of this place which appears destined by nature to be a residence of the Muses. For its attractive situation is immediately apparent, its air is pure and health giving, its provision of every sort of food is abundant and easy, and there is a great wealth of suitable lodging and of the other necessary things. At this time, for the good of the school that we call our own, we have in the last months and at considerable expense, set up classrooms and buildings. We are maintaining them in readiness in that part of the town which of all is the most suitable for this enterprise, for this training-ground of the Muses, or – perhaps more accurately – this workshop of letters, set apart from the din of men and their activities, and in close connection with a roomy and imposing church. This is the outcome of our decision and intention. With the help of Almighty God we hope for success. Our greatest desire it is to serve his glory and the common good. For our part, and commensurate with our strength, we shall not permit anything to be lacking.

edition of Copernicus's *On the Revolution of the Celestial Spheres* with his own commentary. Despite his learning, he was bitterly opposed to the Gregorian calendar. Besides this writing, he conducted autopsies, prepared horoscopes, composed poetry, took care of the library, and twice served as rector. He also continued his physician's practice. Aged sixty-five, Mulerius died of a stroke on Sunday 5 September 1630 and was given the honour of being buried in the chancel of the Academy Church. His son Petrus (1599–1647) was appointed professor of botany and physiology in 1628 (while he had academic virtues, he appears to have been an alcoholic who fought with his students). Today, the Nicolaas Mulerius Foundation is headed by the rector and makes grants to assist the research of Groningen staff.

Cornelius Pijnacker: Ambassador in North Africa

Pijnacker (1570–1645) was the son of Adam van Kerckhoffe, treasurer of the water board of the province of Delft (a significant appointment in the Low Countries) and Johanna van Polanen. The couple descended from old, respected families from a village called Pijnacker a short distance from Delft. At the age of seven Cornelius was sent to a local school where he received his first education. He was given a thorough grounding in Greek, Latin and music. Pijnacker continued his study in Heidelberg in 1590. He was preparing to leave for Geneva when Elbert van Pallant, lord of Selm and Dirsfort (Germany), convinced him to accompany van Pallant on his study tour through Italy, Sicily, Austria, Moravia, Bohemia, and Germany.

After this, Pijnacker returned to Leiden where he decided to study law; he dedicated himself with all his heart to his new subject and received his doctorate in canon and civil law on 16 May 1597. Two months later he started a job as a lawyer. However, he had hardly commenced when he was called back to Leiden and appointed professor after the previous incumbent quit his job for a position at court. At Leiden, Pijnacker married his first wife, Suzanne van Treslong remaining there until 1614, when the States of Groningen and the *Ommelanden* tempted him to come to their newly founded academy. He gave lectures at Groningen and was rector in 1616–17 but in 1622 he was asked by the States-General to go to North Africa on a diplomatic mission to restore peace with the sultan of Turkey, who had stolen 150 cargo ships from the Dutch. He returned from his mission successful and when problems broke out again he was summoned once more to be a member of an embassy in 1625. Because of his absences he had to resign his chair. He did return to academic life though: the States of Friesland gave him a chair in law at the academy in Franeker.

Hermann Ravensberger: Precocious Theologian

Hermann Ravensberger (1586–1625) was born in Siegen, Germany, on 30 September 1586. He specialised in law at the Calvinist academy at Herborn in Hesse and later also at Heidelberg. He then commenced his study of theology, again in Herborn and afterwards at the University of Marburg. He soon reaped the fruits of his labour, and in 1609, aged only twenty-two, Ravensberger got his doctoral degree in theology where he became professor the following year. In 1614 the count of Bentheim entrusted him with teaching theology at his school in Steinfurt and also with the administration of the churches in his sphere of influence. A short time later, Groningen made him professor of theology. Ravensberger worked there for eleven years and published several books in his field. He was the academy's rector on three occasions. A year-long disease that slowly took over his body finally undermined him. He died peacefully on 20 December 1625.

Coat of Arms

The coat of arms of the university has not changed since 1614; it has only been stylised. At the university's foundation, it incorporated the region's coat of arms: two quarters have the Ommelanden arms with its eleven hearts and three stripes, and two quarters have the city's arms with its two-headed eagle. In the centre was an open Bible bearing the motto *verbum dni lucerna pedibus* (this is now *verbum dni lucerna*), an abbreviated version of *verbum domini lucerna pedibus nostris* (the word of the Lord is a light for our feet) from Psalm 119, verse 105. The reference to light also alludes to Wessel Gansfort who was described as 'the second light of the world'.

Distinguished Theologians

By the 1620s the academy needed at least one supplementary professor in additions to replacements for the founding professors who had died or gone elsewhere. Again, the States of Groningen and the Ommelanden were keen to appoint international talent. Some of the most prominent of these were theologians.

Franciscus Gomarus: Hammer of the Arminians

Franciscus Gomarus (1563–1641) was born in Bruges. Because his family were Calvinists they were forced to leave Bruges and they went to the Palatinate in the Holy Roman Empire as its elector, Frederick III, was a devout reformer. At fourteen Franciscus enrolled at the University of Strassburg where he was a student of theology. He subsequently studied at Neustadt, at Oxford and at Cambridge where he received his MA in 1584. Leaving England for Heidelberg, he was awarded his doctorate and he went on to become a pastor at Frankfurt. When he was appointed professor of theology at Leiden he was at odds with the trustees and he engaged in heated public dispute with his colleague Jacobus Arminius (1560–1609) who rejected Calvin's theology of predestination, believing that there was no incompatibility between human free will and divine omnipotence. When all this became intolerable, Gomarus resigned to teach at Saumur in the Loire. Although they already had Ravensberger, Groningen invited Gomarus to a chair of theology and Hebrew, an offer he eventually accepted in 1618. That year he represented Groningen at the Synod of Dort (Dordrecht), a national convocation of the reformed church that affirmed the doctrines of Calvin and rejected the arguments of the Arminian delegates. The synod also concluded that a new Dutch translation of the Bible was required and Gomarus worked on part of the Old Testament for it. In his new job too, he had some tensions with his institution on theological questions. However, he remained at Groningen and the north enjoyed the benefit of a learned and well-published man.

Henricus Alting: Successor

Born in Emden, Alting (1583–1644) spent three of his teenage years being educated by Ubbo Emmius. He became a tutor to Willem van Nassau, Koenraad Lodewijk van Solms-Braunfels, and Philip Ernst von Isenburg at Sedan in France. At this time, he came to know the future Frederick V, elector of the Palatinate and king of Bohemia. When Frederick went to England to marry Elizabeth, the daughter of James I and VI, Alting had the opportunity to travel with him and meet important churchmen such as George Abbot, the archbishop of Canterbury. Back in Heidelberg he was appointed to the chair

Allegory of Gomarus's victory over Arminius (1618)

of theology, which was unusual given that he was only subsequently conferred with his doctorate (1623). In 1627 he took up the chair of theology at Groningen (Ravensberger having died the year before) where he was an elder in the city congregation. He was much involved in distributing charity to Calvinist refugees. One of his students, the pastor Abdias Widmarius (1591–1668), became professor of theology at Groningen in 1646. Ubbo Emmius had evidently founded his own academic dynasty.

Matthias Pasor: Arabist

Matthias Pasor (1599–1658) was born in Herbon in Germany where his father was a professor (he was subsequently a professor at Franeker). In part because of the turbulence caused by the Thirty Years' War, Pasor ended up travelling for much of his teaching career. He taught at Heidelberg and Oxford and in the latter lectured in oriental languages (Arabic, Hebrew and Syriac). There is a reasonable amount of evidence that he knew little about these, but evidently he knew more than others at Oxford at the time. It may have been a relief for him then to have been appointed professor of moral philosophy at Groningen in 1629, a position he exchanged some years later for the chair of theology. He was buried in the Academy Church. One of Pasor's students from his sojourn in England, Edward Pococke, became Oxford's first Laudian Professor of Arabic in 1636. The fourteenth Laudian Professor, Geert Jan van Gelder, was a lecturer in Arabic in Groningen between 1975–98, before going to Oxford from which he retired in 2012.

PRINTING

The printed word plays an important role in the academic world with its professors and students, study and research, traditions and customs. When the Academy of Groningen was founded the printing presses of the city became busier. The importance of carefully prepared printed matter for administration and education prompted the curators to employ an official academy printer. At the time it was obvious that Hans Sas (Johannes Sassius; 1607–51) would fulfil this brief. Sas was the first in a line of printers to deal with disputations, dissertations, orations, edicts, songs, regulations, catalogues, and enrolment lists. Between 1614 and 1872, the academy had fourteen official printers. These experienced the ups and downs of the institution; in good times they had a lot of work, but in bad times they had to find other employment. It was not only the official printers who profited from the academy's presence. Gradually, other printers, publishers, bookbinders, and bookstores were established in the city.

From the beginning, professors played a role in overseeing what was printed in Groningen because Groningen's authorities feared the distribution of controversial or seditious books that were traded every now and then by travelling booksellers from elsewhere. Following a 1614 decision of the senate they were especially vigilant in the fields of religion and ethics.

The first beadle's staff, was made in 1615 on the instructions of Ubbo Emmius. Crafted of mahogany, it is topped by a silver hexagon that forms a base for Minerva. Its sides are engraved with representations of virtues (Temperance, Justice and Prudence), and the coats of arms of the province and academy. A replica is carried in ceremonies today.

CHAPTER THREE

EARLY STUDENTS

THE first lectures were given soon after the inauguration of the academy. Unfortunately, no records of registration were kept during these first months. Official enrolment started with Bernhardus Sutholt from Hamm, Westphalia on 13 March 1615. Enrolling at the academy confirmed that a student would submit to its laws and that he would join the academic community. There were eighty-two students in the academy's first year.

Students had to register with the *rector magnificus* in the Academy Building where the *Album Studiosorum* (Album of Students) was signed. The *Album* was in Latin and shows the date of enrolment, the student's name and usually his city of residence. The register is incomplete, as many students did not bother to enrol formally; based on lists from the period 1620–60, it is estimated that one third of all students were not registered in the *Album*. Incomplete registers were common at every university at the time. International students, for instance, frequently stayed for a short period and thus did not register.

The *Album* also indicated whether a student was enrolled for free, which was usually the case with international students. These may have been refugees and this was indicated by the words *gratis quia exul et pauper* (because the student is a poor exile) or *ob patriae calamitatem* (because of his native country's misfortune). Such students might have had no Calvinist university in their own region. Many refugees also received the *vrije burse* (free bursary), which meant that their board and lodging were paid. The number of bursaries granted to students increased from forty to sixty in 1628 and at least half of the places were reserved for foreign students. Although their numbers were not high, it was clear that the local authorities liked to see international students coming to the city.

TOWN & GOWN

Student life in Groningen in the seventeenth and eighteenth centuries differed drastically from that in later times. These differences can be accounted for not only in terms of the academy's relatively small size, but also because a student had a separate status from a Groningen citizen. It is often said now that students live in their own worlds, but that is not what is meant here. A student was not considered a citizen of Groningen, but a citizen of the academic community. This separate citizenship came with benefits and exemptions from duties and rules that the residents of Groningen had to adhere to. This was not extraordinary; older universities, both in and beyond the Republic, had granted academic citizens privileges alluded to in *The Eternal Edict*. Had Groningen not done this, students would have probably have chosen to study somewhere else.

◄ Groningen student (c. 1700)

Students were exempted from obligations related to the safety of the city. It was not compulsory for them to do military service or participate in the building of fortifications. Students themselves sometimes made an exception in special circumstances, such as during the sieges of Groningen (see below). Student privileges also included financial perks; they did not have to pay all of the usual import taxes. However, much to their chagrin, they were obliged to pay taxes on wine, beer and tobacco, unlike their peers in Leiden and Franeker. In 1616, dissatisfied students even disrupted classes and caused disturbances in the street to attain this privilege. However, they gained nothing and the leaders were punished.

University Seals, 1685-1720

In general, it can be said that students in the seventeenth century dressed in a similar fashion to other people, depending on their class. Foreign students were recognisable because they wore clothes from their native regions. Men at the academy only started to distinguish themselves by their clothing at the end of the seventeenth century. The most recognisable student garment at that time was a sort of tailcoat. This looked like a dressing gown and was not only worn indoors but also to classes and during nights out, which made them easily recognisable.

Students lived at home or in a room in a citizen's house, which they usually rented for a year. They received food, candles, and fuel for the fire from their landlord or landlady for an additional sum of money. They did not always eat in their lodgings; it was quite usual for them to dine together in one of the city's taverns. The founding of the university brought considerable benefits to the inns of Groningen.

A student, especially one of high social standing, was expected to participate in activities that befitted his upbringing. Which activities these were can be seen from notes of credit. For example, there were debts for lessons in dancing, foreign languages, horse riding and fencing, and for using the field for *kaatsen*, an old ball game that is still played in Friesland. Some of these activities brought them to group together, and meeting places at times functioned as some sort of club house for drinking, smoking and playing cards

ACADEMIC LIFE

University education in the seventeenth and eighteenth centuries was not as strictly determined by regulations as it is now. There were no fixed study programmes or durations of study, and those enrolled could follow any public lectures. This freedom encouraged students to attend several universities and it was common practice not to stay longer than a few months at an institution. If a student did not like the lectures of a certain professor or if he tired of the city, he could simply move on to another place. This was especially easy in the Dutch Republic, whose several universities were only a few days' journey apart.

The normal age of a first-year student was sixteen or seventeen, but younger men were common. During the first two or three years' study students followed subjects at the Faculty of Arts. This propaedeutic faculty offered courses in Latin, Greek, Hebrew, philosophy, mathematics and history. Students had to study Latin carefully as it was the official academic language. It was up to a student to decide if he was ready to continue his studies at the theological, legal, or medical faculties. This second phase usually took another two to three years.

Education mainly consisted of attending lectures and there was a distinction between public and private ones. The former were freely accessible to all students while the latter were often held in professors' houses. The first printed timetable from 1647, the *schema lectionum*, showed how classes were scheduled. The academy offered the same programme four days a week (Mondays, Tuesdays, Thursdays and Fridays). The first lecture of the day started at eight o'clock and each day consisted of six hours of lectures. Almost all professors taught two hours a day.

Apart from following lectures, students were expected to participate in disputations. A student defended propositions in a debate presided over by a professor who tried to guide the interchange between the defender and his fellows in the right direction. The point of defending was to practice rhetorical and logical skills, not to present the results of original research. The subjects of the disputations were usually determined by the professor involved. These were further elaborations of what had been dealt with in lectures.

A large part of the life of a student of the academy took place in the Academy Building's inner court. This square, surrounded on three sides by a long gallery with Tuscan columns, was the meeting point for students. They discussed contemporary theological and legal issues, but also other less serious matters.

MISBEHAVIOUR

The primary privilege of the academic community was having its own justice system. This was of great benefit to students, because they almost always received milder punishments than they would have received from the city court. The most important characteristic of the *Forum Academicum,* as the academic court was called, was its objective to avoid bringing dishonour on its members. The Academic Senate feared that if students were subjected to the ordinary court system their reputation might be tarnished and they would lose all ambition, perhaps never becoming useful members of society. This privilege came to an end when the academy became a French imperial university in 1811, and after the fall of the French regime it was not re-established.

The *Forum Academicum* treated both civil and criminal offences that were not normally penalised by corporal punishments or the death penalty. The everyday academic court, the *Senatus Minor,* consisted of the rector, the secretary and two professors. The rector could also choose to deal with minor cases himself. More important criminal cases were treated by the Academic Senate (which consisted of all professors), once preliminary inquiries had been made by the *Senatus Minor*. A student sentenced by the *Senatus Minor* could appeal to the Academic Senate, and after that to the *Senatus Amplissimus*, which also included the curators of the university.

The academic court administered several kinds of punishment. Students were normally only given a warning for misdemeanours. A fine was the usual punishment for more serious offences, the money from which was often divided among the professors. Since fines were the most common penalty, it was not surprising that the professors were accused of self-enrichment, although at times the money was used to support poor students. Even quite serious offences were sometimes resolved by a fine: one student who cut a citizen's nose so severely that it had to be amputated was merely ordered to pay the surgeon's costs and an additional charge.

More severe punishments included confinement to one's room or to the academic

Oude Boteringestraat 36-38: the earliest part of the building dates from the fifteenth century when it was a private house. It was sold in the eighteenth century and served as a city courthouse (the cells are still in the basement) until 1998. It now houses the Faculty of Theology. The seventeenth-century facade was restored in the early twentieth century.

prison. A stay in this jail was seen as a suitable punishment for an offence such as vandalism or causing minor injuries. It could be made more severe by ordering that the prisoner be kept on bread and water. One of the army volunteers of 1665 was given this punishment for attacking and insulting some guards and challenging them to a duel. An order of 1667 stated that no one could bring tobacco, alcoholic drinks or candles to the imprisoned student. It is clear from these instructions that such things probably occurred quite often. It was also quite usual to release students during the winter, because it was too cold.

If students really went too far, they could be expelled from the university. This *relegatio* entailed not only banishment from the institution but also from Groningen, and it was often limited to a set period, just like a regular banishment from the city was. Banishment was used for students who had offended the court by not showing up or by being rude during one of its sessions. It was also a punishment for grave offences: one student was exiled for four years for luring someone into his house and beating him up. A member of the academy who committed an even more serious offence could receive the *relegatio cum infamia*; in that case he was not only banished but also declared to be infamous. One man who was caught seducing young girls was given this punishment.

The most severe punishment was the crossing out of someone's name in the *Album Studiosorum*, making it impossible for him to be readmitted. This was what happened in 1657 to a student who had raped a nine-year-old girl. In the eighteenth century, the court started offering students who faced expulsion the opportunity of taking a more honourable way out by strongly advising them to leave the city: the *consilium abeundi*. This did not mean that the student was not obliged to leave; if he did not do so on his own accord, he was removed by force.

The main problems with students were at night with their drinking bouts and accompanying fights. While citizens suffered the most from these nocturnal outbursts, professors were also victims of the violence. A regular and popular activity during such carousing was the scratching of a foil over the cobblestones, a clear challenge to the city watch. There were some cases of more severe violence against citizens. These tumults continued to occur despite the orders issued by the university. Such behaviour became more infrequent during the eighteenth century, but this probably had more to do with social changes and the decrease in the number of students, than with specific prohibitions or penalties.

Dicing and cards were regarded as troublesome, since these often went hand in hand with arguments. In 1618, for example, a card game between two students and two burghers went horribly wrong when it led to a fracas that ended with one of the students stabbing one of the burghers who died shortly afterwards. The student's name was crossed out in the *Album Studiosorum* and the case was handed over to the city court, but by that time the miscreant had fled.

The reasons for condemning gambling are quite clear, but the fact that acting was also disapproved of demands some explanation. Acting was prohibited because it was held to be an inferior and vulgar activity. It is hardly surprising that this prohibition was breached as well. As early as 1623, seven students received a fine for acting, and twenty-five years later, curators and some preachers complained about the sinful plays students were involved in. They claimed that the plays caused riots and fights in which people were injured. Consequently, the senate issued an instruction which clearly stated that acting was strictly forbidden. Notwithstanding this, a theatre company was established in 1769 that consisted of both citizens and students. Professors admonished the students involved and tried to set them aright but these attempts were unsuccessful, and the company continued in existence.

Arguments between students were often sorted out in duels although these were strictly forbidden. The prohibition on duelling is a recurring theme in the documents of the senate. At first, students who had been caught duelling were given a fine and their foils were taken away. When they were again involved in a duel, a short stay in the jail would follow. When duels continued to occur, the punishments became more severe; transgressors had to pay larger fines and were consigned to the jail for six days. It was only when it became unusual to be armed in public that the practice of duelling slowly died out.

THE BURSE

In the first years of its existence, several students went to the Burse for lunch, dinner, and even for breakfast. The Burse was a dining place for poorer students which had been set up at the establishment of the university. Forty, and later sixty, students could eat there for free or at least with a considerable subsidy. The Burse was situated east of the Academy Building and the street which led to it was soon called *Bursegang*.

The meals served at the Burse sounded good: 'For lunch: warm beer and bread, meat, butter, and cheese. For dinner: milk and bread, meat, roast with potatoes'. However, students often criticised the food; the meat was too raw or spoiled, vegetables were of poor quality and had hardly been cleaned or boiled. They also censured the behaviour of the manager, who, according to them, did not want to listen to complaints: he laughed at them, or even doled out a box on the ear. This set a bad example for the Burse staff who also started to be rude and who refused to do what students asked of them. The diners themselves were not always polite either, although they were certainly expected to live properly and study hard. The recommendation that they no longer be allowed to enter the Burse carrying a weapon may have had problematic incidents behind it.

There were other circumstances which could make eating in the Burse unpleasant. For example, in 1649 the Burse staff was given the instruction that students, who normally had to stay in their places while eating, could stand up during meals to warm themselves in winter. It must have been a very cold place. The building was not always very clean or hygienic. In 1615 the manager had been ordered to change the table cloth weekly and in 1667 it was added that this cloth should cover the entire table. Furthermore, he was to clean the dining hall twice a week.

Whatever improvement might have emerged did not last. The following century , the complaints became so clamorous that in 1772 the senate started an inquiry into the chef's cooking skills. The letter that the senate sent to the curators disclosed some unappealing facts: 'the foods chosen are often of the worst quality, on top of which they are prepared and served in a very unappetising manner; awful bacon with half-raw peas that are half eaten by worms; smelly stock fish with half-peeled potatoes; no wonder students become ill'. To protect the 'privileged youths of the academy', the senate appointed Prof. Martinus Schoock as inspector of the Burse. Between 1787 and its closure in 1813, professors were scheduled to attend the hall daily so they could see, smell, taste, and then judge if the chefs were following the food regulations.

STUDENT ORGANIZATIONS

The lives of students and citizens often intersected; they lodged together, exercised together, gambled together, acted together, and at times fought with each other. However, students did stand out by speaking Latin, by their academic privileges, and in some cases by their wearing particular clothes. There were not as yet any well-organised student societies.

Flood in Groningen, 1686. Although membership of the university separated students from citizens, some hardships that befell the city and province could not be escaped. Etching by Jan Luyken (1698).

The only student organisations at that time were the *collegia nationalia* in which those from outside Groningen were united. These groups were not comparable to the student societies that arose in the nineteenth century, although they probably did have some form of membership regulation. Since the *collegia* were unofficial there are no remaining archives and it is unclear how they were organised. There were several in Groningen: those of Gelderland, Holland, the Ommelanden, Overijssel, Ostfriesland, and Westfalen. The *collegia* seem to have been primarily occupied with drinking and quarrelling with other *collegia*. Students who did not want to join were pressured to do so, and in some cases, if they resisted they were beaten.

It was not odd that students from the same region sought each other's company while studying in an unfamiliar city and providing a social group must have been the main objective of the *collegia*. However, this sociability also had its drawbacks for the academy, so they were eventually forbidden, not simply because of drinking and fighting, but also because they allowed students to defend their interests in an organised manner. In 1616, for example, they pleaded for exemption from taxes. They also defended individual members. At the end of the seventeenth century when the number of foreign students started to decrease, the *collegia* slowly started to disappear.

There were no forms of organised student life again until the end of the eighteenth century, which saw the rise of the *ontgroensenaten*. These groups were meant to introduce first-year students to student life, often in a not so pleasant manner (like some hazings in student societies nowadays). These groups were not strictly organised, but were formed by individual students at different times. Only at the very end of the eighteenth century were they formalised, attaining a hierarchical structure mirroring the Academic Senate's. Such groups are rightly seen as forerunners of those that would be founded in the nineteenth century greatly transforming student life.

INTERNATIONALS

After the enrolment of Bernhardus Sutholt, Phillipus Solbach, a second German student found his way to Groningen. The first students from Austria, Denmark, and France arrived a year later, followed by two Englishmen. After Swiss, Polish, Estonian, Scottish, and Russian students, the first non-European came to the academy; in 1640 an American enrolled, and twenty years later a Brazilian arrived. These were probably sons of Dutch pioneers returning to the home country of their parents. The academy even had special offers for foreign students so that it could compete with universities in Leiden, Franeker, Utrecht, and Harderwijk. They received large discounts on meals in the Burse and there were special student facilities, scholarships, and fee waivers.

Due to religious persecutions and warfare elsewhere on the Continent, many fleeing or banished students found a haven in Groningen. In 1616, the university granted financial aid to three Protestant theologians who escaped from Catholic Münster, and in 1620 it welcomed refugees after the failure of the Protestant Bohemian Revolt against the Habsburgs. Another important reason for foreign students to study in Groningen was the attractive intellectual climate of the Netherlands in general, and due to a period of economic prosperity, the arts and sciences blossomed in the seventeenth century.

Austria **4**	Estonia & Latvia **19**	Hungary **162**	Poland **25**
Czech Republic **16**	Finland **2**	Italy **5**	Russia **4**
Denmark **23**	France **93**	Lithuania **3**	Sweden **23**
Great Britain **11**	Germany **2,145**	Norway **1**	Switzerland **106**

Origins of international students in the first seventy-five years of the academy

From the beginning, the university was strongly internationally oriented. The major part of this group, about eighty percent, was of German origin. Most came from the nearby border regions. The average annual number of enrolments was thirty in the academy's early years, rising to more than fifty in the mid-century. This decreased to roughly twenty foreign students per year between 1670 and the mid-eighteenth century. In the academy's first seventy-five years 3,584 (=57%) of students were Dutch and the remainder came from all over Europe.

Professor Macdowell's importance to British civil war politics lay in his influence on Scottish Presbyterians in the Netherlands (and hence his potential influence in Scotland). Groningen's association with reformed theology ensured that several other Scotsmen ended up in the academy. James Renwick (1662–88) from Dumfriesshire first studied at the University of Edinburgh. He went to Groningen to study theology in late 1682 and was ordained there less than six months later. He was an important member of a Reformed Presbyterian union which linked Scotland and Friesland. His faith involved him in opposition to the king of England and Scotland with the consequence that he was hanged for treason in Edinburgh.

Not all the students who came to the Dutch Republic to study returned home. Just as now, the Dutch government would like to benefit from foreign talent that it has educated. For example, another Scotsman, Alexander Comrie (1706–74) of Perth, studied at Groningen before moving to Leiden where he completed his doctorate in philosophy. He had intended to become a Presbyterian minister in Scotland but instead ended up as a minister at Wobrugge in Holland where he wrote several theological works in Dutch (which are still influential), in addition to translating reformed writings from English.

Several of Groningen's international students went on to have distinguished careers. Samuel Rand (d. 1654), the son of a clergyman from county Durham, who had studied at Cambridge and Leiden, received his physician's degree at Groningen in 1617. He became one of London's most important medical practitioners and later one of the most respected doctors in the north of England. Mobility characterised academic careers at the time, something that was already evident in the travels of the members of the Aduard circle. Thus, Victorinus Bythner (c.1605–70), a Polish student who began his studies of theology at Groningen in 1632 ended up lecturing on Hebrew at Oxford where he published several books on that language as well as on the Old Testament.

BOMMEN BEREND, 1665 & 1672

In the seventeenth century, the Dutch Republic was at war for several years with the prince-bishop of Münster, Christoph Bernhard von Galen (1606–78). When the forces of the bishop threatened to lay siege to Groningen in 1665, many students asked for permission to fight; it must have seemed exciting and honourable to them to defend the city. Their request to form a student company was granted immediately and classes were disbanded. The student company was even given its own banner with the inscription *Deo, patriae et academiae* (for God, country, and academy). Parents and guardians had to be asked for permission since most students were still minors. However, the expected siege did not take place and there was nothing to do other than to keep watch. It seems that the students became bored, since there were several incidents in which they started fights. After two months, they were released from their duties and classes were resumed.

When the episcopal forces threatened the city again in 1672, the students were asked to assist and about 150 joined the *Vrijwillige Studenten Compagnie* (Voluntary Student Company). The Bohemian general, Carl von Rabenhaupt (1602–75), who led Groningen's defence, chose the best soldiers from amongst the student body. The *VSC* was an independent unit in the army: not only did it sing mocking songs about the bishop while standing guard (which not everyone appreciated), it also insisted on choosing its own officers.

When the archbishop attacked the city, he did so with an extraordinary amount of artillery. Due to this extravagant use of explosives he was given the nickname *Bommen Berend* (Bombing Bernhard). Despite the barrage, the student company stood its ground. One member was shot in the chest but survived; indeed, none were killed. After a siege that lasted more than a month, the bishop withdrew. The members of the *VSC* received a silver commemorative medal to thank them for their sense of duty and their courage.

The anniversary of the end of the siege, 28 August, is a holiday in the city of Groningen. Now, there is little sympathy for the poor bishop who was merely engaging in what was then wholly acceptable power politics and trying to push back the borders of what he saw as a dangerous and heretical Protestantism. Von Galen had come from a difficult home life; his parents were Protestant, but when his father was imprisoned for murder and his mother opted to join her husband, the young Christoph passed into the care of an uncle who had the boy educated by the Jesuits. After von Galen alienated his parents by converting to Catholicism he pursued a career in the church. As bishop, he showed that he was a committed churchman by introducing many of the

reforms prescribed by the Council of Trent. He also encouraged education in his dio-cese. He did a fine job organizing the standing army that he established in 1654 and combining military strength with diplomacy through careful strategic alliances with England, France and Cologne. However, he had no luck in the Low Countries whence he was twice repelled. Some improved generalship on his part, or a little less resistance from the citizens, would have realized the parallel universe where there is a Von Galen university in Groningen.

CHAPTER FOUR

LIBRARIES

A library is the heart of every university and therefore on 25 February 1615, the City and Province of Groningen decided to remodel an old library into a larger one for the academy. To secure its success, they provided money for new books and other expenses. The old library had been situated in the suppressed Franciscan monastery. The location was favourable as it was in the city centre and just across the street from the academy. This was convenient as, in addition to serving the academy, the library admitted local clergy, civic officials and judges as readers.

The Latin school, the St Martin School, had been located in the Lady Sywen Convent since 1595, but only in the south and west wings of the building. In the unused east wing, the *Bibliotheca* was housed on the first floor. It quickly became clear that the library needed more space and the southern wing was added. To enter the library, you first had to pass through the Academy Church: the stairs leading up to it was in the choir and this was the main entrance until 1829 (see illustration on page 8).

THE FIRST COLLECTIONS, 1615–69

Nicolaas Mulerius was the inaugural librarian (a role he occupied between 1619–21 and 1625–30) and he made the first catalogue in 1619. At this time, the greater part of the Academy Library consisted of recently printed books; a little over 40% of the 400 volumes were printed in the sixteenth century while the remainder dated from 1600. Although Groningen was not a centre of the book trade, the city and academy had organized the purchase of a founding collection. The surviving records provide information on what was valued and taught in the first syllabuses. The collection consisted of core works of reference such as Bibles, glosses and biblical commentaries along with collections of civil and canon law and their associated commentaries (which were frequently large and expensive tomes). The library's biggest collection, that of theology, contained the then standard works of the church fathers along with the sixteenth-century reformers who would be expected in a Protestant foundation: Martin Luther, Philip Melanchthon, Jean Calvin, Ulrich Zwingli, the Centuriators of Magdeburg and Theodore Beza. There were also books (in Latin) by English Protestant authors such as the Cambridge men William Perkins (1552–1602) and William Whitaker (d.1595) and the *Opera* of the local Regnerus Praedinius. It was important to be aware of opposing viewpoints, so the collection included writings by Pope St Gregory the Great and St Thomas Aquinas along with recent Catholic champions such as Francisco Suarez SJ (1548–1617) and the formidable cardinals Caesar Baronius (1538–1607) and Robert Bellarmine SJ (1542–1621).

In 1622 the Academic Senate proposed to the city council that it add the library of the Martinikerk to the academy's library. The Martinikerk's collection included the contents of Catholic libraries that had been seized after the Reduction of 1594. The council agreed and the library's collection grew extensively. Besides this acquisition of several hundred books, the collection was augmented by purchases, bequests and donations

◄The 1864 library with its book store (built 1898) on the right

from the city, the province, professors, students, and others who felt connected to the academy. Atypically, one of these early gifts came from a woman: Susanna van Ewsum gave a German Bible.

In its early decades the books in the library were all chained and students were forbidden to use them. This changed in 1655 when students were permitted to visit on Wednesdays and Saturdays, but only between 12:00–14:00 in winter and between 13:00–16:00 in summer. When the chains were removed is unclear, but they were no longer in use in 1664, when the librarian, Tobias Andreae, asked the university curators for advice on replacing missing ones. In 1668 the library had its locks changed and imposed new, stricter, regulations. From then on, each user had to register borrowed books in a ledger. His name would remain there until they were returned; this was the library's first lending system.

Reading room of the 1864 library designed by J.W. Shaap

The 1668 regulations remained unchanged until 1815. These included a detailed description of the librarian's tasks and obligations. They also prescribed that every inaugurating professor had to donate a book and should provide the library with a copy of every book that he wrote. In the beginning of the seventeenth century, the library was dependent on gifts and grants from the province. At that time, the collection mainly served as a supplement to the professors' private collections. Moreover, the library itself did not have much money to spend, so purchases were rare and relatively inexpensive. However, the 1668 regulations put some pressure on the professors to augment the collection and this allowed the library to grow faster. Furthermore, people who visited for the first time had to pay one silver shilling. General readers were not allowed to take books home with them; only librarians and professors had this privilege. Interestingly, the regulations also stated that an alphabetical catalogue should be made. This might seem obvious now, but until then the books had been categorised in the order in which they were acquired, making it difficult to find them efficiently. Gerhard Lammers (1668–1716), a professor of medicine, who served as librarian for a remarkable forty-eight years, produced the first printed catalogue in 1669.

In 1672 the library was faced with an unusual threat: during the siege of Groningen by the bishop of Münster several houses caught fire and it was endangered. The senate discussed whether they should move all the books to the north of the city where they would be safer. In the end, they decided that this would not be necessary, but they ordered buckets of water to the library and sent two students to keep watch there at night. Fortunately, the library did not catch fire and the books remained unharmed, but Lammers must have mused about what the allocation of two students and their buckets said about the extent to which his collection was valued.

The Eighteenth & Nineteenth Centuries

At the beginning of the eighteenth century the development of the library stagnated. It was not until 1727 that times changed for the better and its collection grew once more. The library was given an annual allowance by the province of 250 guilders. Under the care of Leonard Offerhaus it acquired many precious works and received many gifts. The collection grew to the extent that it was now in need of more space, so it expanded into parts of the west wing of the Academy Church.

After this period of growth, the library went through difficult years again. New journals and new branches in the sciences appeared, but it could not afford to keep up with them. When King Louis Napoleon planned to visit Groningen in 1808, the senate formulated the need for funds for the library, but the royal visit never happened. When the academy came under the direct control of Emperor Napoleon in 1810 things got worse as the annual allowance from the province ceased.

In 1813 the French retreated, the United Kingdom of the Netherlands was founded, and better times arrived for the library. For example, in 1816 a few of its rooms had stoves installed. Security was also improved: until 1823, more than twenty people had library keys and supervision was lax so it was not surprising that many books went missing. Thereafter, the curators changed the locks and there were only two keys. Professors still had to be able to access the books when they wished, and this was achieved by using an assistant known as the amanuensis who was given free accommodation near the library.

After this brief revival, the cycle of funding decreased again. All the faculties wanted to have a say in how the subsidy provided by the province should be spent, and professors started to speak up about crucial books that they felt had to be present in the collection. Disputes between the library, the university and academics were common, especially since the subsidy was cut back. New purchases had to be postponed, cancelled, or paid for by future revenues, and the books in the library were neglected.

In 1835 a new librarian was appointed: Petrus van Limburg Brouwer, professor of Greek, Roman antiquities and history (in addition to which he was a novelist). Brouwer wanted to improve the collection and he dealt with all the troubles that had been piling up during the term of his predecessor. As enrolment figures grew, so did library funding, and its debts were paid off. What followed was a modestly prosperous period with improvements made by Prof. Willem Adriaan Enschedé (1811–99). The subsidy of

> ### Paper Books
>
> 1620: 400
> 1853: 30,000
> 1898: 85,000
> 1914: 170,000
> 1965: 850,000
> 1986: 2,000,000
> 2014: 3,000,000

the province stabilised, allowing the library room to grow. In 1852 it was decided that students could borrow books once they registered. The opening hours were extended: on regular days it opened between 12:00–14:00, and on Mondays and Thursdays it opened between 15:00–16:00. Enschedé also recatalogued everything, giving the cabinets, shelves, and books corresponding numbers.

1864 library

However, the building in which the library was housed was deteriorating quickly. Cracks were showing, stones were falling out, and the façade was in danger of collapse. The building was supported with struts and later even had to be evacuated, so the senate decided to build a library. This new facility was opened on the site of the current University Museum in 1864, the first purpose-built library in a Dutch university. It had been designed by Jan Willem Shaap (1813–87) who had been influenced by the British Museum. This library witnessed two notable changes, the installation of electricity in 1904 (which allowed it to remain open much longer) and the appointment in 1900 of Jan van Haarst, the first full-time librarian.

ADDITIONS & DEACCESSIONS, 1919–2013

During the nineteenth century the book collection had grown substantially and at the beginning of the twentieth century it became clear that new facilities were necessary to keep up with this. It was decided that the building of 1864 would be taken down, and in its place a new one would be erected. This new building was completed in 1917 but officially opened two years later. Its architect, Jan Vrijman, had designed the Academy Building.

Predictable setbacks followed due to the financial crisis in the 1930s and the Second World War, but after the liberation of the Netherlands, the library picked up where it had left off at the beginning of the century and soon suffered from lack of room again. Moveable shelves were introduced to create more room, and new departmental libraries were founded so that many books and journals found their way out of the central building.

The number of students and books kept growing and the need for space became increasingly pressing. The university acquired adjacent land in the late 1960s and the library was remodelled between 1968 and 1972, one of the many changes overseen by W.H.R. (Wim) Koops, the librarian between 1964–1990. More storage room was added in the late 1970s by using other buildings. Nevertheless, the building could not keep up with its growth. A plan was made in 1966 to construct one large central library with several large departmental libraries to replace all the smaller ones. At this time, the curators investigated whether the entire university (or parts of it) should move to the Paddepoel area in the north of the city. While discussions were held and investigations were carried out to decide this, the question of the library's accommodation stagnated. It was not until 1983 that planning for the new building designed by Prof. Piet Tauber (1927–2017) could be commenced. History repeated itself, as the library once again took over a disused Catholic building, this time the neo-Gothic St Martin's Church (1895) designed by Pierre Cuypers, the architect of the Rijksmuseum. Although there were reservations about demolishing this landmark, it had not had a congregation for decades and so the library took its place, opening in 1987 at Broerstraat, no. 4. This is essentially the structure of the current library, but a quick tour of what it looked like before its recent renovation can be taken on YouTube by looking at *The University of Groningen Lipdub* (see Vries, 2011 in the Bibliography for the URL). That Tauber's building has lasted so long is a tribute to its design. Now, in a time when libraries are changing so rapidly, to conceive a library from scratch is to invite the judgement of posterity on your short sightedness.

A decade after Tauber's library opened, the computerised catalogue was completed. To mark the occasion the Board of the University presented the library with a 4x10m abstract painting by Gerriet Postma whose vibrant colours relieve the starkness of the great stairwell that runs the height of the building. In contrast to the labour of cataloguing, Postma spent an entire day on his work, preferring spontaneity to planning. It is, perhaps, better than it sounds.

The computerised catalogue is now something taken for granted. The more obvious recent computer-related change is a large investment in electronic books and journals. At the time of writing, there were over 580 database subscriptions across all disciplines. In common with the printed collection, these represent the international scope of research at the university. For some disciplines these electronic resources will render a physical library almost obsolete.

Before Tauber's building was itself renovated, the library system underwent substantial changes. Some of the separate faculty libraries (e.g. Arts and Theology) were reabsorbed from their external sites back into the central building. Even after multiple copies of individual books were disposed of and books were sent to the library's repository in Zernike, this increased the pressure on space for books on open shelves. Some of this was eased by removing volumes and journals that were available to users electronically through their library membership. Some of this was eased by sending books that were not often used into storage. However, these logical solutions were supplemented by the decision to cut back the open access shelving of items only available in paper format so that, for example, to browse an encyclopedia, a reader may have to call up thirty volumes. Even to find a particular entry you have to order two or three volumes (as it is not always clear which one has the entries for P for example). Perhaps more importantly, there was no longer a core collection of work on the shelves to browse.

This was a step in a significant shift in library priorities. Having gone from an extreme where only professors were allowed to borrow (or sometimes steal!) the books when the library was first founded, the priority became the provision of study spaces of various kinds (including rooms for group study). For a while in 2013, about a fifth of the public part of the main floor was taken up by a 'learning grid' whose colourful couches, beaded curtains and large screen monitors cost many thousands of Euros before it disappeared in the exigencies of the last renovation.

SPECIAL COLLECTIONS

The library houses the Centre for Russian Studies (opened 2010), a Korea Corner (2014) and an extensive Documentation Centre for Dutch Political Parties (1973). As well as these, the library has a separate Department of Special Collections that looks after a wide variety of precious texts that do not fall under any straightforward unifying description. These include early modern documents from the university's printers, medieval manuscripts, the eighteenth-century Crijnsz

collection of pamphlets on religious controversy, the Staverman collection of translations and adaptations of Daniel Defoe's *Robinson Crusoe* (1719), and a variety of historical maps. One noteworthy treasure is an edition of Erasmus's *New Testament* from 1527 which has been annotated both by the hands of Martin Luther and Groningen's Regnerus Praedinius. These often unique items require a care more typical of a museum, but with the difficulty that the objects being preserved must be made available to readers. Papyrus, parchment and paper all require different handling. The books about 'old books' take up several shelves in the Special Collections reading room, testament to the training required for their safekeeping.

Digital Collections

The library hosts an ever-growing digital collection of high resolution images of its own holdings of special interest. These are freely available online through an English interface, *Digital Collections* (see Bibliography). Here one can find an unpredictable collection of ancient and medieval manuscripts, maps, letters and examples of Dutch commercial bookbinding (1890–1950). An annotated facsimile of Nicolaas Mulerius's *Syllabus Librorum Omnium in Bibliotheca Academica Groningæ & Omlandiæ*, the library's first catalogue (1619) is also online (see Bibliography). The library participates in other digitization programmes, co-operating with Google Books and the Royal Library in The Hague to preserve out-of-copyright Dutch texts. As part of its commitment to open access the library provides the platform for a variety of free academic journals such as *Ancient Narrative*, *The International Journal of Personal Psychology* and the *eJournal of Indian Medicine*.

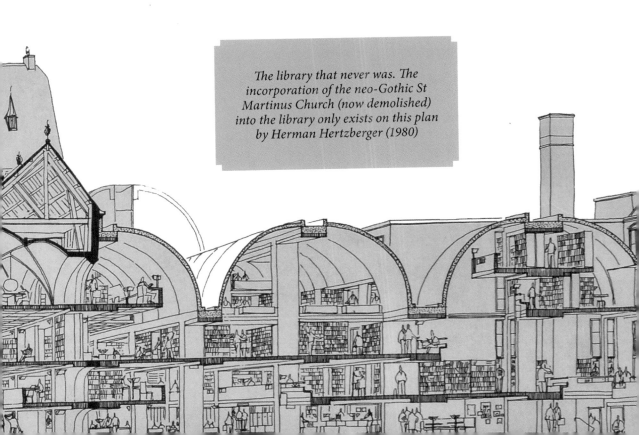

The library that never was. The incorporation of the neo-Gothic St Martinus Church (now demolished) into the library only exists on this plan by Herman Hertzberger (1980)

RENOVATION, 2014–17

The central library was renovated between 2014 and 2017 in accordance with a design by AG Architects of Haarlem. Given the building's site, there was no room for expansion. The consequent transformation was remarkable for many reasons. The most obvious of these was that the original plan had a 2020 finishing date, but it was decided to accelerate the process so that it became a rare example of a major project that was completed well before time. To achieve this while maintaining business as normal (or as near normal as possible), library staff repeatedly moved the open collections without succumbing to the despair of knowing that these were merely temporary measures while the final building layout was achieved. Part of the new layout involved the convenient relocation of the issue desk to the ground floor. There, a user can be rewarded not only with any books she ordered, but with the opportunity to witness a wholly automated borrowing and return system that defies practical computing laws by working simply and correctly regardless of the size of the volume being processed. The renovation also included some more predictable but no less useful elements: there are more plugs for laptops, improved ventilation and a fresh, spacious atmosphere conducive to study. The building now has 300 solar panels and an A energy rating. The director of the library, Marjolein Nieboer optimistically concluded that 'The UL is future proof!'

◄ Minerva: a window (1919) by L.F. Asperslagh in the Vrijman library, now the University Museum

The inclusion on the site of a Starbucks was somewhat controversial, particularly for those who were unhappy about the reduced tax that the company paid to the Dutch exchequer. The decision to install a coffee chain on the premises was odd, but peripheral. Certainly, no-one could complain of being forced to purchase refreshment from there as the city centre is full of cafés. Furthermore, the renovated building includes coffee areas on each floor. As the architects stress, for students these are: 'the ideal place to take a break, discuss something, and "see and be seen"'. This inclination to catering has expressed itself in some diner-style booths in the reading rooms (where people are theoretically silent). The design decisions are in keeping with the study-space model that had been in operation since before 2014, one that measures success in terms of the number of people who pass through the doors, rather than in terms of the number who wish to use to the library as a library. There are currently 2,100 study places and 290 'break seats'. To these will be added a bicycle garage when the bookstacks in the basement are removed along with the last pretensions to be a research facility.

For now, the University Library is based in three locations, the renovated site opposite the Academy Building, the Central Medical Library in the UMCG and the library at the Zernike Complex in the Duisenberg Building.

PETRUS CAMPER

CHAPTER FIVE

1700-1814: ENLIGHTENMENT

THE second century of the academy's existence was marked by several problems: the number of students declined, staff vacancies were not filled, and the budget was limited. However, the history of the eighteenth century was not all negative for the academy. Some of its most famous professors taught during this period, men such as the historian Leonard Offerhaus and the physician Petrus Camper. Furthermore, at the end of the century, the academic hospital was established (Chapter 6).

PUGNACIOUS BERNOULLIS

In 1695 the Swiss Johann Bernoulli (1667–1748) was appointed to the chair of mathematics in Groningen on the strength of his work on calculus. Bernoulli incorporated practical demonstrations into his lectures (including a pneumatic pump and a Leiden jar) and thereby attracted a charge of heresy for his pains. For a decade the university had one of the world's greatest mathematicians on its staff until he quit his post to succeed his brother Jakob (1654–1705) as professor at Basle. Johann's son, Daniel (1700–82), who had been born in Groningen and who was the founder of hydrodynamics, trained in medicine and was also appointed professor at Basle, first to the chair of anatomy and botany, and then to the chair of physics. Another son, Johann Jr (1710–90), succeeded to his father's mathematics chair (despite having a doctorate in law). The Bernoullis were a family as much divided as united by their mathematical abilities. The brothers Johann and Jakob quarrelled so much professionally that when in 1699 they were simultaneously admitted to the Académie Royale des Sciences, it was on condition that they ended public squabbles that were dragging their discipline into disrepute. Daniel's success provoked jealousy in his father. It is likely that Johann Sr would have been unhappy that the Bernoulliborg, a building opened on the Zernike Campus in 2008, commemorates both him and his local-born offspring. He has, at least, the consolation of Henk Ovink's untitled 1996 galvanised steel sculpture on the road from the city into the Zernike Complex. The work commemorates Bernoulli's brachistochrone curve, the solution to a mathematical problem he himself had posed exactly three hundred years earlier (see page 150).

CRISIS

In the late seventeenth century, enrolment at the Academy of Groningen fell. Between 1705 and 1715 the average number of new students in a year was thirty-five (with low points in 1708 and 1712 when there were only 23 first years). One explanation for this was the decrease in international students coming to the Dutch Republic in consequence of the wars with France and England. Another explanation was the lack of new professors. No new professors were instated between 1706 and 1714, leaving several positions vacant. This had terrible consequences for some departments: all three chairs in the Faculty of Theology were vacant for five years between 1712 and 1717. In 1714,

◄ Petrus Camper by Marie-Anne Collot (1781). Presented after Camper cured her daughter of chickenpox, the bust survived the Academy Building fire of 1906

Bernoulliborg (2007)

the year of the centenary celebration, there were only four professors left: Alexander Arnold Pagenstecher (1659–1716) in law, Adam Menso Isinck (1668–1727) in rhetoric, Theodorus Muyckens (1665–1721) in medicine and the aged Gerhardus Lammers (1642–1719), who had been appointed in 1667, a physician.

The failure to fill chairs was due to arguments in the States-General between the Ommelanden and the city. When the city asked for the finance for new appointments, the Ommelanden stalled, declaring that they were not yet ready to decide the matter. Because of this, the centenary of the university was not celebrated. Things recovered a little after 1717. In February of that year the Ommelanden finally agreed to the appointment of new chairs. However, new this did not result in an immediate increase in the number of students: in the seventy-five years after its foundation (i.e. 1614–89) the academy enrolled 6,231 students (of which 3,548 were Dutch and 2,683 were from abroad) whereas in the 119 years between 1689 and 1808, there were only 5,659 enrolments (4,371 Dutch and 1,288 international).

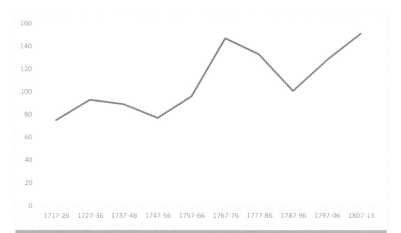

Numbers of doctorates conferred at Groningen between 1717–1813

Orange-Nassau

Between 1740 and 1748, most European countries were involved in the War of the Austrian Succession. This fact, combined with the poor military results of the Dutch army, plunged the Dutch Republic into an economic crisis. When France invaded Flanders in 1747 and again in 1749, the people called for a prince of Orange to govern the Republic. Because of this unrest, Willem IV, already stadtholder of Friesland, Groningen, Overijssel and Gelderland, was appointed stadtholder of Holland, Zeeland and Utrecht. At the same time, stadtholdership became hereditary. Willem IV obtained a great deal of power, not only in national politics, but also at the Academy of Groningen. In May 1748, he was named *rector magnificentissimus* and *primus curator* of the academy. In 1749, the prince came to Groningen to formally take up his new duties. However, the more important reason for his visit was the changes he wished to make to the administrative organisation of the province.

Willem V visited the city of Groningen on several occasions. One of his visits took place in the summer of 1773. On 19 July 1773, the senate was informed that the prince would visit in August. Immediately all professors and students who were away on vacation were called back. The programme was similar to that for the royal visit in 1749. The professors used this opportunity to ask for privileges that Willem IV had previously promised. They understandably wanted some of the advantages enjoyed by professors at other Dutch universities (for instance, those in Franeker received 150 guilders in tax compensation each year, and members of Leiden had to pay less duty on wine). Prince Willem replied that he could not decide the matter on the spot, but he promised to take it into consideration. However, the same requests were repeated in 1777, confirming that the petition had not been successful.

Making History: Leonard Offerhaus

Leonard Offerhaus was born on 18 November 1699 in Hamm, Germany. He went to the gymnasium in Gouda and then to the Athenaeum of Deventer. In 1723 he commenced his studies at Utrecht, where he attended classes in theology and history. A mere two years later, he was promoted to professor of history and classical languages in the chair of philosophy at the College of Lingen, Germany. Lingen was experiencing troubled years at the time and before the arrival of Offerhaus the chair of philosophy had been unfilled for almost three years.

In 1728, Offerhaus moved to Groningen. He was not the first professor from Lingen to receive an offer from the academy: between 1717 and 1724, three others preceded him. In his inaugural lecture he outlined the development of Christianity in the first centuries, arguing that this church slowly developed into what he regarded as an anti-Christian, papal church. The topic of the lecture was carefully chosen. It reflected the greater importance attached to theology than to history. He would not be teaching history to aspiring historians, but to future clergymen.

From 1744 Offerhaus was also librarian of the university (see page 33). To his teaching of classical languages and history he added geography and Roman antiquity. Surviving syllabuses show that in 1748 and 1750 he taught a chronicle of world events up to the Peace of Westphalia in 1648. In 1750 he adopted a different system and covered creation to Charlemagne, followed the next year by Charlemagne to 1700. It is not surprising that he produced a two-volume *Compendium Historiae Universalis* (1751) which he dedicated to Willem IV. This book was used in several Dutch and German universities. When Willem IV died, the Academic Senate decided that rather than the *rector magnificus*, it was Offerhaus who should deliver an oration.

In 1752, Offerhaus became responsible for teaching Dutch history. Another professor took over his courses in Latin, making Offerhaus the only professor in the Netherlands whose sole responsibility it was to teach students history (he covered general, Dutch, and Roman history). His last published work (1763) was about the Low Countries. In 1778, he celebrated his fiftieth year at Groningen, an event that was honoured with a procession, a public lecture, music and a banquet. He continued to work until his death on 18 October 1779, when he was a month short of eighty.

Offerhaus's salary did not reflect his position. At the start of his career in Groningen he earned 1,000 guilders a year. When he took on the post as librarian, he received an additional 200 guilders annually. According to a report from 1750, there was only one other professor earning less than Offerhaus. On becoming professor of Dutch history, he received a pay increase of 500 guilders, bringing his total income to 1,700 guilders a year. In the past, few academics got rich.

NATURAL SCIENCES

The natural sciences became increasingly popular in the eighteenth century, both in academic circles as well as in the better-off classes of society. The eighteenth century can even be characterised as the age of science. The public was fascinated by experiments and self-educated men conducted their own. This interest resulted in the establishment of several learned societies at the end of the eighteenth and in the early nineteenth century. Such societies and the academic community often collaborated and thus encouraged scientific development. There were three important eighteenth-century movements that contributed to the study of science at the time: the Enlightenment, empirical philosophy, and physico-theology.

Enlightenment ideas created an ideal atmosphere for the popularisation of the natural sciences. While a scientist is now almost always specialised in one area, an eighteenth-century one did not limit himself to a single or even to a few disciplines. Continuing the humanist tradition of the *homo universalis*, he spread his attention across scientific fields, across mathematics, physics, chemistry, astronomy, anthropology, zoology and botany. One of the best examples of the *homo universalis* was Petrus Camper; few were as accomplished in several areas as he was. The Enlightenment scientist focused more on the practical use of science than on its theoretical development. This need to be of use to the world was typical of eighteenth- and nineteenth-century academics.

The increase in attention to and popularity of the natural sciences was in part due to new theories of empirical philosophy. Abstract rationalist thinking, as seen in some of the writing of René Descartes (1596–1650), was slowly being replaced by the empirical approach of John Locke (1632–1704) and Sir Isaac Newton (1642–1727). Descartes believed that the basic principles of mathematics and physics were innate, and that people could develop these sciences in their minds using reason alone. Already in the seventeenth century there had been countercurrents to such Cartesianism. Scientists such as Francis Bacon (1561–1626), Newton and the brilliant Irish chemist and physicist, Robert Boyle (1627–91), tried to base science on more empirical grounds, and in the eighteenth century observation and experiment became more important than *a priori* speculation.

The two Leiden professors Willem Jacob 's-Gravesande (1688–1742) and Petrus

Musschenbroek (1692–71) were the most influential Dutch empiricists of the time. Their influence would reach Groningen only in the second half of the eighteenth century. Empirical philosophy had been introduced by the mathematician Jacob Bernoulli, but he had been opposed by many people, particularly by theologians. It was not until Petrus Camper was appointed professor in 1763 that empirical philosophy really started to gain ground. Spectacular experiments caught the attention of the public, and scientific theories were often quite comprehensible to lay people.

Another reason for the increasing popularity of science was the rise of physico-theology, or natural theology. This stressed learning about God on the grounds of the book of nature (supplementing the Bible), an approach which might appeal to St Paul for support: 'For since the creation of the world God's invisible qualities—his eternal power and divine nature—have been clearly seen, being understood from what has been made' (Romans 1:20). Scientific enquiry thus became vital to everyday life. This can be summed up in the title of John Ray's *The Wisdom of God Manifested in the Works of Creation* (1691). An eighteenth-century Dutch scientist did not need to oppose revelation or reason. Instead, the more knowledge there was of science, the more knowledge there was of God's wisdom. Again, a popular book title puts this succinctly, this time one by Bernard Nieuwentijt, which can be translated as *The Right Use and Contemplation of Nature, for Convincing Atheists and Unbelievers* (1715). Physico-theology thus greatly contributed to the popularisation and flourishing of the natural sciences and remained very influential in scientific thinking in Groningen. It would not fully disappear until the twentieth century.

Homo Universalis: Petrus Camper

Camper (1722–89) was one of the most celebrated Dutch academics of the eighteenth century. He was an all-round scientist who conducted important research in areas such as anatomy, zoology and medicine. On top of that, he was an accomplished illustrator, a much-appreciated writer and speaker, and a politician. He is thus rightly described as a *homo universalis*.

Camper grew up in Leiden and as a boy took private lessons in painting and engraving as well as studying perspective, skills that later stood him in good stead when he was recording his scientific findings. More unusually for a son of a wealthy family, he practiced woodwork and welding which later allowed him to design medical instruments. He began at the University of Leiden at the age of twelve, and there he was conferred with doctorates in two subjects: medicine and philosophy. Afterwards, he undertook the customary travel through Europe, visiting cities such as Paris and London. He had three professorial appointments, at Franeker (1751–55), Amsterdam (1755–61), and Groningen (1763–77). At Franeker, he married Johanna Bourboom, the widow of the mayor (who had been his patient). After his time in Amsterdam, during which he was a very active physician, surgeon, obstetrician and professor, he returned to Friesland and spent three years on his estate, researching, publishing and fulfilling political duties.

Camper assumed the professorship of medicine, surgery, obstetrics and botany at Groningen in 1763. He said that his time in the city was the happiest of his life. He became involved in public health issues such as vaccination against smallpox, since he wanted to be of use to society. He also introduced several new surgical instruments and operation procedures. His scientific views were quite outspoken; he dismissed Linnaeus's taxonomic system and greatly disliked the popularisation of science.

Camper had always been very involved in obstetrics, and over the years focused on problems where the head of a baby got stuck during birth. He thought it possible that such babies could be delivered by severing the cartilage connecting the mother's pubic bones. There were two important questions to be asked: would the connection knit back together and would the woman be able to walk again? He performed the experiment on a pig and it worked. He was anxious to try the experiment on a woman, and even tried to save a lady condemned to death on the condition that she should submit to the operation. This was not allowed however (and the malefactor was beheaded). Although he tried his utmost, he never actually got to perform this experiment 'necessary to mankind' on a living subject. Less controversially now, he objected to the execution of girls who had been found guilty of infanticide, pointing out that they were often victims of older seducers: 'I do not plead for the crime, but for humanity'. He also championed the establishing of orphanages as a concrete measure for reducing infanticide.

In 1773 Camper ended his career in Groningen, but he remained active in science and politics until his death in 1789. His reputation as a brilliant scientist and a person who cared about society lives on to the present.

ALL OF US ARE BLACK, 1764

On 14 November 1764, Camper delivered a lecture *On the Origins and Colour of Black People* in the anatomy room. Despite the fact that much of what he said does not accord with modern science, it remains a remarkable document. Skin pigmentation was something Camper had long been thinking about. Although he said that he was interested in this solely as an anatomical question, he makes larger deductions that were contrary to widespread prejudices of his day (slavery was not abolished by The Netherlands until the mid nineteenth century).

Camper was amazed at the poor science of even august men who claimed that the blood and brains of black people were black, something that ran counter to all observation. Commenting on one of these scholars he observed:

He probably would have thought in a friendlier and more reasonable way if he, as we do in our country, had seen black people every day and had seen that white people, men and women, however superior they may feel to those coloured people, do not judge them unworthy of their love.

Oude Boteringestraat 44, which now accommodates the Board of the University, was built in 1791 for J. van der Steege, a wealthy physician who had returned from the Dutch East Indies. The building preserves twelve eighteenth-century oil paintings of rural scenes in wooden wall panels.

Camper rejected the suggestion that, unlike white people, black people were akin to apes. Instead he asserted, 'all of us are black, only more or less'. He could have said that all of us are white too, as he argued that the skin of all people is layered, that the first layer is white, that this is covered by a layer that can be 'black, brown, red-copperish or tanned' and this in turn is covered by a layer that is transparent. The pigmented layer is never the same colour life-long all over the body and although there may be different reasons for this, the principal one is tied to generations of exposure to the sun. He concluded that skin colour is irrelevant to determining who was descended from Adam (who might have seemed 'black, brown, tanned or white'), and thus for determining who was part of the human family.

In an aside on how strange white-coloured people must look to others Camper noted that after the savage destruction wrought upon them by Europeans, the native people of America may have believed that white was the colour of divine displeasure: 'All of us, not only as human beings, but as Christians, would wish to be black if we could wash off this sin through such a change in colour'.

WAR & REVOLUTION, 1780–1805

The Dutch Republic was again involved in a war between 1780 and 1784, namely the Fourth Anglo–Dutch War. After three victories, the English struck back by seizing hundreds of Dutch merchant ships, thus nearly stopping Dutch trade. People blamed Willem V's policy for the defeat. One of the main complaints was that the prince had too much power. Local governments and a newly arising groups of democrats, mostly consisting of merchants and craftsmen, adhered to this opinion and these were known as the patriots. Opposing these were the supporters of the house of Orange. In 1785, the stadtholder and his family fled to Nijmegen out of fear of persecution by the patriots. Two years later a Prussian army arrived in the Netherlands at the request of Willem V's wife, Wilhelmina, the sister of King Frederick William II of Prussia. The Prussians brought the rebellion to an end. Although patriots remained in the southern Netherlands, many fled the country.

University mace, 1811-13

The arrival of the Prussians led to renewed enthusiasm for the royal family. Citizens of Groningen wore orange bows to show their support for Willem V. In October 1787, the Academic Senate informed students that they could participate in this 'orange craze', but that they should employ decorations with moderation and as their status demanded. In 1789, the municipality of Groningen declared that all people in government positions had to follow the Dutch constitution, which allotted a great deal of power to Willem V.

It added that professors had to be careful about voicing criticism of the royal government. Everyone was to contribute to the peace in the Republic and those refusing to do so would be removed from office. The Academic Senate responded, deciding to have all professors sign a document pledging that they would not act as agitators.

The year 1789 was also the year of the French Revolution. Revolutionary armies commenced a campaign in Europe, and the Dutch Republic was attacked by the French army which crossed the frozen rivers on its borders in 1795. The invaders were joined by Dutch patriots. Having had some practice, Willem V fled, this time to England, and the Dutch Republic was reformed into the Batavian Republic (from the name of part of the Netherlands in Roman times), a French satellite that suffered badly against the British navy (losing colonies and the battle of Camperdown, 1797). This republic witnessed two 1798 coups (in January and in June), followed by another in 1801. In 1805 the French replaced the government with a president and council, an arrangement that lasted less than a year.

Two Bonapartes, 1806–13

The Netherlands became a monarchy in 1806, when Napoleon's brother, Louis, was crowned king of Holland, a throne he occupied until 1810 when he was forced to abdicate for siding too much with his people's rather than the emperor's interests. In August 1808, there were rumours that the new monarch would visit Groningen. However, Louis

postponed this journey and instead visited the province of Drenthe. The Academic Senate decided to send representatives there to deliver compliments to him. They feared a drastic reorganisation or perhaps even a suppression, since Louis had granted Leiden the title of Royal University of Holland, while Utrecht and Groningen had to make do with their titles as academies. Nevertheless, no changes had been made by 1810 when the Netherlands were officially incorporated into the French empire.

In 1811, Emperor Napoleon visited the Netherlands, but the Academic Senate decided against sending a delegation to greet him. The local authorities tried to convince them otherwise, but to no avail; the senate would wait for the emperor to visit their city. Napoleon never arrived in person, but on 30 June he sent an inspector, Georges (subsequently Baron) Cuvier (1769–1832), the celebrated naturalist and a member of the council of the Imperial University (which, though based in Paris, regulated education in all French territories). Cuvier was greeted courteously and given everything he required, which included the academic regulations, a list of professors and other staff, a set of financial accounts and a report – in French – of the state of the institution. He was evidently satisfied because on 22 October 1811 Groningen became an academy of the Imperial University. It did not gain anything by this; indeed, it lost some of its independence as the government installed new administrators. However, it did better than Utrecht, which lost its academy status, and Franeker, which was closed down.

Eredoctoraat

An honorary doctorate (*eredoctoraat*) is conferred on someone of academic distinction or on someone who has given significant service to society. In some Anglophone countries it is also used for fundraising. Groningen has awarded honorary doctorates since 1717 when Rev. Abraham Trommius was given one for his work on a concordance to the Bible. The latest conferral (2018) was on Ban Ki-Moon, former secretary-general of the UN, for his contribution to peacekeeping and the environment. In between, about 200 people were honoured, five in the eighteenth century, almost forty in the nineteenth and over sixty in the bicentenary year of 1914. A more restrained ten were given to mark the celebrations in 2014.

After Trommius's degree, a Swedish-born German, Christian Reichsadel (1696–1775), received a doctorate in law since which time a significant number of recipients have been international ones. A dozen names give a flavour of Groningen's international links:

1843: Karl Gützlaff, a German evangelical described as the 'apostle of the Chinese' and now regarded as one of the most controversial missionaries of all time. Answering directly to God (having abandoned the restrictions of the Dutch Missionary Society), he went as far as acting as interpreter for opium smugglers so that he could disseminate more Bibles. He was a talented linguist who published on China and who wrote fifty tracts in Chinese. Selfless and sincere, he reinforced Chinese opinions that Christianity and imperialism were linked.

1884: Robert Koch, the German founder of bacteriology identified the causes of tuberculosis, cholera and anthrax. As a teenager he had to repeat a year in school and, despite a lack of obvious linguistic gifts, he wanted to study philology at university. For a while it was possible that the young man would become an apprentice in a shoe shop or emigrate to America. Luckily, he and his family eventually decided that he would study science at Göttingen. He travelled to India, New Guinea and Equatorial Africa to explore his theories and was active in treating patients as well as in advising the government's department of health.

1914: Sir William Peterson, a Scottish classicist, was a canny administrator and the first principal of University College Dundee before moving to Montreal to become principal of McGill University: 'he found a group of largely autonomous schools and transformed it into a university'.

1914: The Parisian clinician Prof. Pierre Janet was one of the most famous men in his field. He studied philosophy at the École Normale Supérieure at a time when the discipline was merged with psychology and he went on to qualify in medicine with a thesis on hysteria (which he held to be a mental rather than a physiological problem). In one memorable case, on encountering an unresponsive patient who behaved as if he was possessed by the devil, Janet proceeded to address himself to Satan. The man revealed that he had been having an affair. The therapist's cure was to help his patient forget 'the prerequisite to moving forward, to progress, to life itself'.

1914: Svante Arrhenius was a Swedish Nobel Prize winner in chemistry (for his work on ionic theory) and, subsequently, director of the Nobel Institute. Two of his ideas which did not weigh in his favour as a candidate for an honorary degree at the time were panspermia (that claim life on earth was due to spores from another part of the universe) and global warming.

1914: Prof. Sir Edward Albert Sharpey-Schafer was the discoverer of adrenaline and the founder of endocrinology. He added 'Sharpey' to his name as a mark of gratitude to the founder of a scholarship he benefited from at University College, London. In furthering his research on nerves, he deliberately cut one of his own in his arm. He was noted for his support of the admission of women to study medicine.

1921: Annie Jump Cannon was an American astronomer known for classifying stars. She succeeded in a scientific career despite being deaf and being a woman at a time when Harvard was very wary of female academics (she did not get a normal academic appointment until 1938, three years before her death).

1989: Andrei Sakharov was a Russian physicist who worked on the USSR's nuclear armaments. He subsequently questioned the morality of this and began working for human rights with the result that he was exiled. He was awarded the Nobel Peace Prize in 1975. The European Parliament's first Sakharov Prize for Freedom of Thought was awarded to Archbishop Desmond Tutu in 1988.

1999: Helmut Kohl was one of Europe's best known politicians, the chancellor of Germany and the architect of its reunification. He had a PhD from Heidelberg in modern history. The year he received his honorary doctorate he also received the American Presidential Medal of Freedom. However, 1999 ended on a bad note as he was forced to admit that he had accepted anonymous and therefore illegal political donations. Somewhat embarrassingly for the university, Kohl was not available to come for the conferral until 2000 by which time some questioned whether the honour should be withdrawn.

2009: Hisashi Owada (1932–) is a former president of the International Court of Justice and Japanese representative to the OECD and the UN. His academic career included teaching at Tokyo, Harvard, Columbia, NYU and Leiden. His recent retirement may be related to his daughter's imminent ascension to the Imperial throne (she is married to Crown Prince Naruhito).

2012: Archbishop Desmond Tutu (1931–) is an irrepressible Nobel Peace Prize laureate and theologian. His fame as a defender of human rights in Apartheid and post-Apartheid South Africa is world wide. In addition to his work on behalf of the dignity of all people regardless of race, he has taken strong stances on a wide range of issues including climate change, the treatment of the Rohingya in Myanmar, the right of people to assisted dying, and homophobia ('I would refuse to go to a homophobic heaven. No, I would say sorry, I mean I would much rather go to the other place').

It should be admitted that not every doctorate conferred by the university was wholly without some self-interest. The 1914 degrees included the steel magnate and philanthropist, Andrew Carnegie and Princess Wilhelmina. The latter made a generous and enduring gift to the university when she became queen (see page 100). Half a century later, her daughter, Queen Juliana (1909–2004) also received a doctorate (page 110).

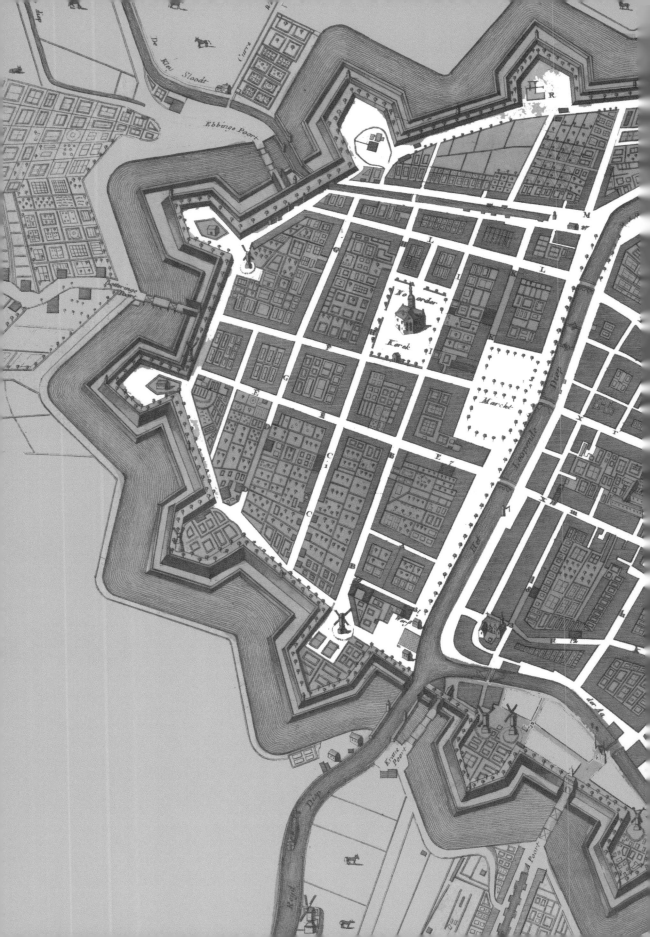

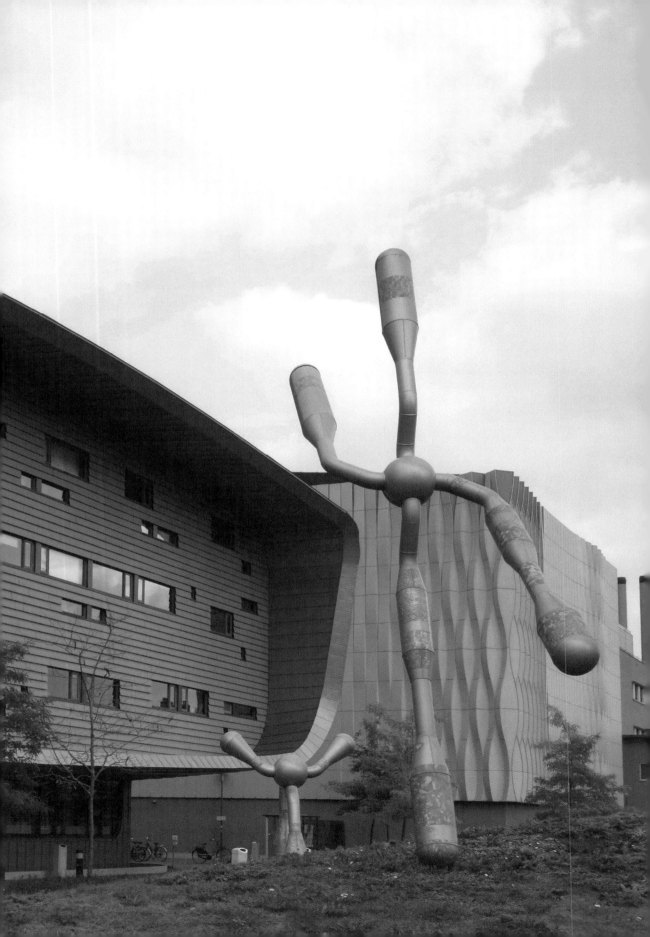

CHAPTER SIX

MEDICINE

THE new academy had a sound beginning in the seventeenth century, but out of the four faculties that of medicine was the smallest and perhaps the least appreciated one. Nicolaas Mulerius was the first professor of medicine. He was also in charge of teaching anatomy and preferred to emphasise practical education. He therefore used the old convent – where the University Museum is currently located – to establish an anatomy theatre. There were, however, few dissections carried out during Mulerius' time, and after his death the theatre was hardly ever used. This changed in 1647 when Antonius Deusing (1612–66) became professor of medicine. He sought precise explanations of nature and valued the practical as well as the theoretical in education. His whole life was spent quarrelling with charlatans who had no scientific or theological backgrounds. The anatomical theatre, which by that time had fallen into disuse, was rebuilt in 1654.

Deusing left the actual anatomy education in the capable hands of Henricus Eyssonius (1620–90), who was appointed professor of anatomy in 1654. Eyssonius brought autopsies back into the study programme even though this progressed slowly due to the paucity of corpses. There was still a repulsion against autopsies, and executions – a source of bodies – were rare. Eyssonius was an advocate of a hands-on education. He was the first to argue for the foundation of an academic hospital. He suggested turning part of an orphanage into a clinic, since Groningen did not have a hospice that could be converted into an actual hospital (as had happened in Utrecht and Leiden). He wanted to treat poor people of all ages and sexes, with the quid pro quo that the bodies of patients who died in the hospital might be used for dissections before they would be properly buried. At the same time, Eyssonius suggested that the language of instruction be changed from Latin to Dutch. He also envisioned exams for midwives. However, his ideas were not embraced by the university authorities.

In 1763, more than seventy years after Eyssonius' death, Petrus Camper became professor of theoretical medicine, anatomy, surgery and botany at the university. He started a *Collegium Casuale Chirurgicum*, a practical course in which he treated actual people. Before his departure in 1773, Camper had treated five hundred patients and student numbers had trebled.

CORPSES

Wouter van Doeveren (1730–83), a professor of medicine in the late eighteenth century, was very interested in anatomy and, until the arrival of Petrus Camper, he was responsible for anatomy classes. During his time in Groningen, he frequently lamented the lack of corpses for study. Most of these cadavers were shipped in from Amsterdam, but this was problematic during cold winters. This led van Doeveren to overstep his boundaries. In 1762 a hatter complained that someone had desecrated the grave of his daughter. The local church started an investigation and a man was arrested. This detainee declared that he had exhumed the little girl at the request of van Doeveren,

◄ *XY* by M. Borchet, (2009) with UMCG research lab and power plant in background

who had paid him two guilders. Van Doeveren was interested in the girl because it had been rumoured that she had a double spine. The desecrater was banished from Groningen, but there is no record that the city, church or university took steps against van Doeveren.

Current Dutch law allows people to give their bodies to medical science. The UMCG only accepts corpses of people who have died in the previous 24 hours. A corpse must be free of infectious diseases and cannot be obese. When the anatomy department have finished, the remains are cremated and the ashes are spread at sea. Who volunteers for this? A Dutch study of 2010 surveyed 765 registered donors: men and women were represented roughly equally, 79% of respondents listed no religious affiliation, 25% were involved in health care and 11% in education. Most donors (93%) explained their choice in terms of being useful after they died and 49% wanted to show their gratitude to medical science. More unusually, 15% disliked the idea of burial or cremation and one person even wished to avoid being of any financial benefit to funeral companies.

THOMASSEN À THUESSINK & THE GREEN ORPHANAGE

Evert Jan Thomassen à Thuessink (1762–1832) was appointed professor of medicine at Groningen in 1794. Three years later he proposed to change the city's The Green Orphanage into a *Noscomium academicum*: an academic hospital where students could be schooled in recognising diseases and treating patients. The university urged the city to agree to Thuessink's plans. The resultant hospital was located in two arched rooms, one for women and one for men. Each was furnished with four beds with hair and wool mattresses and a pillow. Thuessink himself decided which patients would be treated. He selected those who were 'the most suitable for my students'. The initial expense of nearly 700 guilders was higher than the 500 guilders he had budgeted for. In addition, the university had to pay the orphanage for the rent for two rooms which came to a total of 600 guilders a year. However, the university was not responsible for the day-to-day care of the patients. The orphanage had to provide them with decent food and drink, fire, light and clean linen. These tasks were performed by the 'mother' and 'father' of the ill who had to answer to the medical professors.

From letters written by a student, Jacob van Geuns, it is clear that Thuessink held two public consultation hours each week. Van Geuns also mentioned that the classes at the hospital comprised eight students. He complained that it was difficult to find the right patients, because some were not suitable for their teaching objectives, while others did not wish to be transported to Groningen. Yet in June 1798, van Geuns proudly wrote to his father that about sixty patients had been treated during the academic year.

THE MUNNEKEHOLM HOSPITAL, 1803

After the enthusiastic start in 1797, problems began to arise. There were ongoing financial issues, it remained difficult to find the right patients, and the hospital was too small. In 1801 a suitable alternative was found: the former West-Indies House on the Munnekeholm. The financial situation of the Batavian Republic hindered the move, as did developments surrounding the military hospital housed in the Prinsenhof (in 1803 it had to relocate, and one option was to transfer to West-Indies House). Thuessink opposed this plan; he argued that merging his hospital with the military one would lead to logistical problems. Moreover, the patients that were treated in the military hospital were not suitable subjects for students, and their very presence might scare off regular patients.

Munnekeholm & Micturating Man (1786)

The new hospital on the Munnekeholm was finally opened at the start of the academic year 1803–4. Again, it was a small two-room institution with eight beds. This hospital is often regarded as the first real academic hospital in Groningen because it had its own building and directly employed its staff. In its first year, eighteen men and eighteen women were treated, only one of whom died (of dropsy, a swelling of soft tissues due to the accumulation of excess water). A mere five students attended the practical classes. The following year, fifty-five patients were treated, thirty-one men and twenty-four women (of which four died). At the end of 1804 the hospital opened its own pharmacy and Thuessink happily reported that they had acquired a bath. The Munnekeholm site was expanded in 1808 after the arrival of Johannes Mulder, a doctor who specialised in midwifery and surgery. Mulder demanded three more rooms, a surgery, a delivery room, and a room for wealthy patients. A room for wealthy patients may sound odd. During his stay in Groningen Mulder treated several people who afterwards made donations to the hospital. These were more than welcome, and thus Mulder requested a special room for them. After all, patrons could not be placed in the same room as the indigent.

In 1810 the hospital received over 5,000 guilders from the government to separate the clinic for internal diseases from the one for external diseases. Part of these funds was later used to build an operating room. Five years later, the hospital again received money from the government, this time 4,500 guilders. Four new rooms were furnished, two for external diseases and two for midwifery. Additionally, an operating room, and a consultation room were built and two bathrooms were constructed. The latter were not only used by patients, but also by private individuals, who paid a small amount to take a bath.

APSAZ MERGER, 1851

After the grants of 1810 and 1815, the hospital again struggled with financial problems. There was too little money to properly furnish the hospital; indeed, there was not even enough to pay for groceries. During the summer of 1819 it was rumoured that it would have to close but Thuessink and his colleagues managed to make ends meet. Even in later years, when the hospital received more money from the university and the government, it remained difficult for it to avoid going into debt.

The academic hospital and the municipal hospital for the poor (established in 1820) were amalgamated in 1851 under the name of the General Provincial, City, and Academic Hospital (*Algemeen Provinciaal, Stads- en Academisch Ziekenhuis* or APSAZ). The city hospital was located on the Popkenstraat and had room for fifty patients. The academic hospital on the Munnekeholm was rebuilt and joined to the former building of the Natural History Museum. After remodelling, it housed 124 patients, a great improvement, but the Faculty of Medical Sciences wondered whether it would be sufficient. The hospital was again enlarged in 1861 when the city bought an adjacent building for the treatment of prostitutes. On several occasions, the city rented other buildings so that they could treat people with contagious diseases. For example, in 1832, 1849 and 1866 Groningen suffered from cholera epidemics: in 1849 approximately 700 people died within a short period of time.

Munnekeholm Hospital (1903)

NOCTURNAL DISTURBANCES

In 1873 someone being treated at the hospital was discharged in the middle of the

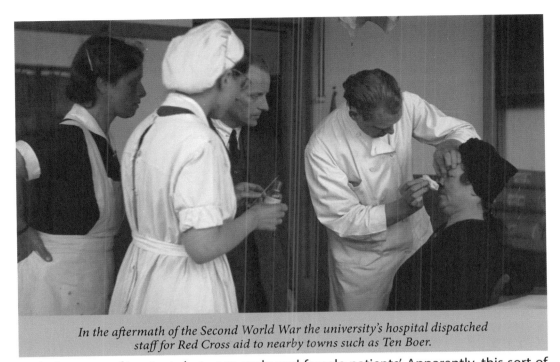
In the aftermath of the Second World War the university's hospital dispatched staff for Red Cross aid to nearby towns such as Ten Boer.

night because of 'contacts between male and female patients'. Apparently, this sort of thing happened more often, and, just as bad, some of the staff were intoxicated on the job (around 1870 the 'father of the ill' and the pharmacist were both fired for this reason). Predictably, medical students also caused problems. In 1872, for example, the police made note of the misbehaviour of several students and a midwifery assistant. The nature of the misbehaviour remains unclear, but it involved the daughter of the resident dry nurse. Dr Julius Jacobs, the brother of the celebrated Dr Aletta Jacobs (see page 77), was fired from his job as an assistant because he had entered the room of the wet-nurse's fifteen-year-old daughter during the night (he was discovered after tripping over a woman sleeping in the same room).

Nurses' Lives

During the nineteenth century important changes took place among the hospital staff. In 1890 the first nurses were trained: they would gradually replace the assistants and the 'mother of the ill'. Four women began on the first course but only one completed it. A year later, four new students started but again only one finished the year. Nevertheless, from 1895 onwards, the number of trainee-nurses and nurses grew significantly. These first nurses were responsible both for the patients and for the cleaning of the hospital. At the start of the twentieth century, nurses worked according to the following timetable: at 6.30am the day-nurses started their shifts. Around 8.00am they had a thirty-minute break to eat breakfast. A second breakfast followed at 12.30pm. Between 4 and 5pm dinner was served after which the nurses had half an hour for recreation. The night-nurses started at 7.30pm and then the day-nurses were free to go out until 10.30pm (except for the first-year nurses as they had to remain indoors).

Nurses worked seven days a week, twelve hours a day. They had one day off every two or three weeks, but only if the number of patients allowed it. Consequently, they did not have a lot of time for relaxation. When they did, they lacked many options. In 1916 the hospital tried to provide them with more possibilities than merely walking in the garden. It contacted the Harmony Theatre, which agreed to allow nurses, at no cost, to visit shows that were not sold out. Nurses were housed in a building belonging to the hospital and had to follow the house rules, some of which now appear curious: they were not allowed to have matches, candles, lights, strong-smelling soaps or perfumes in their possession, and they had to take a bath at least once a week.

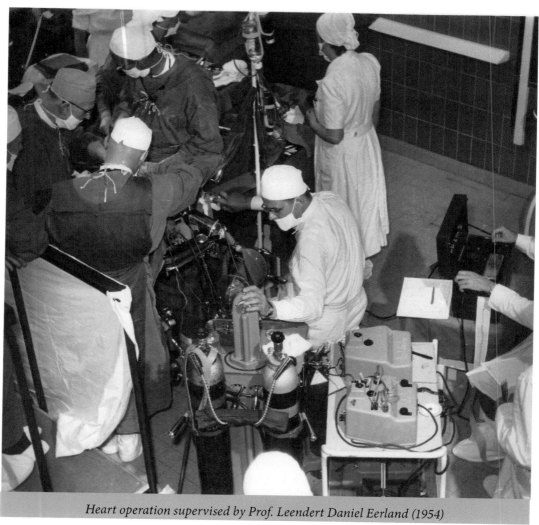

Heart operation supervised by Prof. Leendert Daniel Eerland (1954)

THE OOSTERSINGEL, 1903

Several documents describe the deplorable state the hospital was in during the later nineteenth century: the rooms were too small; the number of beds per room was too high; the heating and ventilation were bad; there was no pharmacy; patients with chronic, curable, incurable and contagious diseases could not be properly separated; during cold winters all sorts of people used the hospital for shelter; the building was not cleaned properly; the food was poor; students were not properly guided, and so on. In 1865 Samuel Siegmund Rosenstein (1832–1906) was appointed professor of medicine. He made plans for a brand-new hospital to be built either outside the old city walls or south of the city. However, no action was taken until 1893 when the government decided that the new hospital would be located on the Oostersingel and would have 350 beds. This new facility was opened on 29 May 1903. The building had cost approximately two million guilders. In its first weeks the public could have a look inside for a small payment and this garnered the hospital 1,296 guilders.

At the start of the twentieth century, the hospital distinguished between three classes of patients: third-class patients were placed in wards, second-class patients were in two-bed rooms, and first-class patients enjoyed the luxury of a private room. The family of first-class patients could have dinner at the hospital and healthy family members of a first-class patient could also stay if a patient requested this. Additionally, the affluent could bring their own nurses.

All meals were prepared in the central kitchen. This was furnished with nine boilers, the largest of which had a capacity of 350 litres. It was staffed by a head chef, five assistants and a potato peeler. In 1936 the old kitchen was rebuilt. The floor area trebled, and the total capacity of the boilers went from 1,550 litres to 5,600 litres. Patients of different classes received different meals. The menu for a first-class patient consisted of soup, two meat courses, two types of fresh vegetables, dessert and wine. The menu for a third-class patient was much plainer and consisted of meat, farinaceous foods (oven-baked dishes made of leftovers, including flour), legumes and soup. Fruit never appeared on their menus and they were hardly ever served potatoes.

During the twentieth century, the hospital was expanded several times. As branches of medical treatment developed, new buildings were attached and older ones were altered. For example, a clinic for ophthalmology (1932) and a paediatric ward (1941) were added. This was possible because of the original structure of the hospital. It had not consisted of one building, but of several independent constructions with green belts in between. The hospital on the Oostersingel incorporated fifteen different structures: administrative buildings and a pharmacy, a medical ward, a surgical ward, an obstetric ward, the director's office, a psychiatric ward, an isolation hospital, the mortuary, the domestic building (including the kitchen), filter beds for biological cleansing, a coalhouse, a loading and unloading space, a workshop, a block for laboratory animals, and a boiler house. The most significant changes to the buildings were made towards the end of the century when the current building on the Oostersingel was constructed.

Plans for a new hospital on the Oostersingel were drawn up in the 1970s after the institution became the Academic Hospital Groningen (*Academisch Ziekenhuis Groningen*, AZG) following an act of parliament that had emphasised the importance of hospitals to education and research. In early building ideas the structure of the new hospital was quite like that of the 1903 hospital; namely, a set of independent buildings with their own entrances. In later plans, the hospital consisted of only one building, with a single main entrance, a central reception desk and covered passageways.

SEXY SCIENCE

The Neuroimaging Centre opened in 2003. It provides facilities for functional magneto-resonance imaging (fMRI), electroencephalophagy (EEG) and transcranial magnetic stimulation (TMS) in the service of brain research and clinical studies. Neuroimaging is used by several disciplines including cognitive science, linguistics, neuroanatomy and neuropsychiatry. Current projects involve the investigation of depression, multiple sclerosis, Alzheimer's disease, schizophrenia and fatigue.

One of Groningen's most exciting experiments involving MRI pre-dates the Neuroimaging Centre. In a 1999 paper in the prestigious *British Medical Journal* a team based in the hospital described their MRI scans of heterosexual sex. Previous attempts to explore the physiology of arousal had been premature as the appropriate technology had not been available. However, the Siemens Vision MRI machine (into which individuals are usually inserted on a small table, and which makes some people claustrophobic) was only 50cm in diameter so careful planning was needed. Other obstacles were surmounted with some doses of Viagra (only a couple who were amateur street acrobats 'trained and used to performing under stress' managed adequate coitus without this assistance). The results showed that many previous physiological assumptions about genital changes in women and men were incorrect. In 2000 the authors of the paper were awarded the Ig Nobel Prize for medicine. The prize is awarded for improbable research that makes people laugh and then think. It was an innovative use of new technology that had had to battle against predictable initial doubts before receiving the permission to proceed.

European Institute for the Biology of Ageing (ERIBA)

As part of its research commitment to the theme of healthy ageing the university established the European Institute for the Biology of Ageing whose first director, Prof. Peter Lansdorp, was appointed in 2010. Its mission is to 'understand the mechanisms that result in aberrant functioning of old cells and tissues in order to develop evidence-based recommendations for healthy ageing.' With the prospect of an older population in the Netherlands and the consequent increase in medical expenditure, the institute focuses on molecular mechanisms that could lead to fundamental breakthroughs in the long term rather than on quick fixes for current problems. It is one of a handful of institutes in the world with this research agenda.

Minus 80°

After a construction period of fifteen years a new hospital was officially opened in 1997. On 13 January 2005, *de Brug* (the Bridge), was completed, connecting it to the Faculty of Medical Sciences. The opening of the Bridge coincided with the fusion of the hospital and faculty into the UMCG (*Universitair Medisch Centrum Groningen*, University Medical Centre Groningen). One of the current building's most striking features is its internal streets that allow patients and visitors to maintain an element of normalcy in their lives by visiting a café, buying a book or some pastries. Building of new facilities for teaching and an animal research laboratory on the north side of the hospital were completed in 2007. A proton-therapy facility treated its first oncology patient in 2018. To save space in the centre of the city, the hospital has logistic and storage facilities at Eemspoort on the outskirts of Groningen. Here, 13,000,000 samples are stored in a robotically operated freezer at −80° centigrade.

The UMCG bears scant resemblance to the original two-room, eight-bed hospital of Thuessink. Over the centuries, the number of beds has increased beyond the imagination of the eighteenth century. The Oostersingel had 350 beds in 1903, 700 beds in 1953, and 1,100 beds in 1978. This became 1,339 beds after the reconstruction. The UMCG is one of the largest hospitals in the Netherlands and the largest employer in the north. It deals with over 30,000 admissions annually, performing nearly 1,000 open-heart surgeries in addition to transplants of bone-marrow (1,651), kidney (152), liver (56), and heart and lungs (37). Its 2017 report lists more than 12,700 employees and 3,400 students (educated as physicians, dentists, and movement scientists). The UMCG is one of the most pervasive and concrete benefits of the university to the city and province that nurtured it.

CHAPTER SEVEN

1814-1914: EDUCATION ACTS

THE military defeats of 1812 and 1813 brought an end to the French Empire and in November 1813, Willem VI of Orange was proclaimed sovereign prince of the United Netherlands. The university felt that it had reason to celebrate its bicentenary and Willem VI was invited to the festivities. He not only accepted, he also donated 1,400 guilders for their organisation. On 9 October 1814 the royal party arrived in Groningen where they were offered the silver keys to the city. The next day official celebrations started early in the morning with a service in the Martinikerk after which the party moved on to the Nieuwe Kerk. There, the *rector magnificus* gave a Latin speech on the origin and accomplishments of the university. At the end of the day, about a hundred people were invited to dinner. Following this banquet, a masquerade of printers and booksellers took place and then a gala theatrical performance. The celebrations continued the second day in the absence of Willem (who had left for Leeuwarden). The city was again splendidly lit and at night a masquerade of students took place.

MASQUERADES

Before masquerades came into being, students organised serenades for important occasions such as royal visits. These were non-costumed parades in which students paid musical homage to an important person such as royalty or the *rector magnificus*. This was common before 1814, and in the nineteenth century it became a recurring event every time a new rector was inaugurated. After the bicentenary of the university, masquerades came into being alongside the serenades. These portrayed an historic or allegorical event which required costumes. The origins of these costumed parades might be found in the triumphal entries held to celebrate victories in Ancient Rome. The masquerades developed from being spontaneous dress-up games, to historically accurate outdoor plays in which the parade itself retained only a minor role.

The 1814 masquerade was entitled 'Priests of Minerva'. Students formed a procession in the costumes of Roman horsemen, gods, and Minerva herself, accompanied by music and song. They set out from the courtyard of the academy, holding a hundred torches to light the way which led through decorated streets. In the process, a serenade was held at the mayor's house, and the evening was concluded with a dinner paid for by students for specially invited guests. The following century saw twenty-four student masquerades. In the first half of the nineteenth century they were held for the inauguration of a new *rector magnificus*, but from 1864, when students took over the organized of festivities, the main reason for masquerades became university lustrums.

THE ORGANIZATIONAL DECREE OF 1815

When Napoleon escaped from exile and re-entered Paris in triumph, decisive measures were called for and, in March 1815, Willem declared himself king of the Netherlands before the emperor and his army moved into the south of the country. This external

◄*Student dressed as Sir John Child of the East India Company for the 1859 masquerade* threat reconciled a country that had internal tensions (north and south, Protestant and Catholic), and 25,000 Dutch fought under the command of Prince Willem (later Willem II) in the army led by the Irish general, Wellington, at Waterloo on 18 June 1815.

When the French were finally defeated, Willem I made reforming higher education one of his priorities and this resulted in the Organizational Decree of 2 August 1815. This involved the issuing of new statutes to three universities, Groningen, Leiden and Utrecht. The decree reduced the power of local trustees in favour of that of central government and placed the monarch at the system's head. The Organizational Decree dictated that higher education was to prepare students for 'a learned rank in society'. In doing so, it ran counter to the French emphasis on utility. The decree established that a university was not intended to prepare men for professions and it was not to provide technical education. To ensure this, the decree specified which subjects pertained to which courses. Latin was to be the *lingua franca*. Students who took a *kandidaatsexa-*

1815 Syllabus

Arts: Greek, Latin, Ancient Greek history, Roman history, general history, logic, Dutch literature, mathematics, and physics.

Law: Greek literature, Latin literature, logic, mathematics, general history, legal history, the *Institutes* of Justinian, Roman law, Dutch law and natural law.

Medicine: Greek literature, Latin literature, logic, mathematics, physics, botany, dissection, physiology, pathology, pharmacy, natural history, medicine and comparative anatomy.

Science: Greek literature, Latin literature, logic, science, physics, astronomy, natural history and botany.

Theology: Greek, Latin, Hebrew, Oriental literature, Dutch literature, Ancient Greek history, Old Testament history, general history, mathematics, logic, ethics, natural theology, church history and Christian doctrine.

---

men were faced with a syllabus with an obviously classical core.

The *Almanac* of 1816 shows how students experienced lectures: 'In every professor's class you are writing steadily during the lecture, with barely time to take another pen from the supply of fresh ones every now and then, or to stretch your crooked, ink-stained fingers – my occupation the whole morning'. The student who wrote this added that in the evening he had to spend many hours trying to make a clear text out of 'the only partially legible, irregular and often messily written pieces'. Professors must have been hard at work too, since they were obliged to teach more than one subject.

Steam: Sibrandus Stratingh

Sibrandus Stratingh (1785–1841) was professor of chemistry and technology at the University of Groningen from 1824 until his death. He conducted important research in the field of motion and became famous for an experiment that truly fascinated people. In 1834 he made a test drive through Groningen of a steam-driven vehicle that he had designed himself. The experiment was widely covered in the newspapers, and Strating could count Willem I as one of his admirers. The king even visited his laboratory during

a royal visit. Stratingh figured that with some small improvements to his design the vehicle would also be able to drive on cobbled streets.

REVOLTING BELGIANS, 1830

The 1830 July Revolution in France triggered riots in Brussels. The short-lived United Kingdom of the Netherlands had been riven by internal tensions and north and south were divided by religion and the unequal distribution of political influence. Willem I prevaricated and the military expedition he eventually sent south crystallised division without bringing any victory. At the outbreak of the Belgian Revolution, 115 Groningen students, nearly half of the university's total, volunteered to serve the king. When they were leaving the city they were given a banner to march with (which is on display in the upstairs hall of the Academy Building). The students formed part of the 8th Infantry Regiment. Their campaign was a brief one, so the brigade that returned the following year had suffered only one casualty and that was from illness. In the meantime, France, England, Prussia, Austria and Russia had decided to recognise the state of Belgium and guaranteed its neutrality.

Dutch honour was slighted but many northerners did not otherwise lament the loss of the southern states and the reduction of the country's population to three million. Although the king accepted that Belgium would become a separate country, the terms on which this was to happen occupied him for a decade during which he alienated many of his subjects, with the result that in 1840 he abdicated in favour of his son, Willem II.

TRUTH IN LOVE: PETRUS HOFSTEDE DE GROOT

The part that the university played in the Netherlands was not principally a military one. An important contribution to nineteenth-century Dutch culture was provided by the Groningen school of theology which was gathered around Petrus Hofstede de Groot (1802–66; appointed professor in 1829) and the journal *Waarheid in Liefde* (Truth in Love). As well as lecturing, de Groot preached to capacity crowds in the Martinikerk. The Groningen school stressed practical morality rather than abstract dogma and believed that the Enlightenment had had a deleterious effect on Reformed Christianity. It sought to unite the Dutch people in a national tradition that looked to Wessel Gansfort and Erasmus. Predictably, this approach was rejected both by Calvinists who held to the importance of the beliefs of the period of the Dutch Revolt, and modernists or liberal Protestants, who saw reason as playing a key part in religious matters.

STUDENT NUMBERS

Although initially the university recruited students from a broad northern geographic catchment (including Germany), this eventually shrank to the point where only students from its province and a small section of the rural area of Friesland were enrolled. Locals' loyalty decreased, especially from the 1860s onwards. Reasons for this included greater mobility (provided, for example, by the national train network) and that Ostfriesland, which had been part of the Netherlands, was incorporated into Germany by Napoleon. In Ostfriesland, High German became the mandatory language for schools

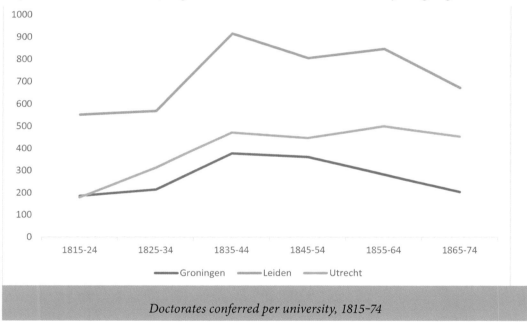

Doctorates conferred per university, 1815–74

and Dutch Bibles and church books were banned. The result was that the number of students from the area who attended Groningen plummeted and by 1855 the flow had dried up completely. Other regions, such as Reiderland and Bentheim, underwent similar developments, leaving Groningen out in the cold.

From mid-century, the number of students from Friesland and Drenthe decreased as well. Many explanations have been given for this. It has been suggested that the Frisians left because the university was struggling, or that the elite oriented themselves towards the southern universities while only rural inhabitants remained in Groningen. In the latter respect it is important to note that whilst a united country had been established in 1798 and re-established in 1815, before a constitutional amendment of 1848 The Hague's influence was limited, but afterwards political power became much more concentrated there. As a result, the upper classes began to focus strongly on the western cities rather than Groningen.

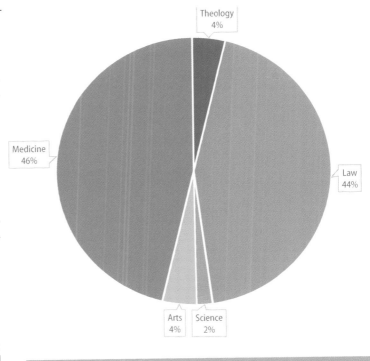

Theology
4%

Medicine
46%

Law
44%

Arts
4%

Science
2%

Doctorates conferred per faculty, 1815–74

At this stage it was rumoured that the government considered the three universities of Leiden, Utrecht and Groningen too expensive, and that Groningen was vulnerable since it had the fewest students (in 1865 it had had 206, but that number declined to 142 four years later while Leiden and Utrecht had 500 and 400 students respectively). The situation in the Faculty of Medicine was most precarious. Investments could not be made to improve the deplorable state of the hospital at the Munnekeholm and the government would not provide funds to employ more professors. In 1866, Prof. S.S. Rosenstein, who originally came from Berlin, had only accepted his chair on the condition that the hospital was to be renovated. What was promised him was only partially fulfilled. Thus, when Rosenstein was presented with the chance to become a professor in Leiden he did not hesitate to move. This was a major blow to Groningen, one aggravated by the fact that many students followed him.

The decline in student numbers slowly reversed with an influx of men who were not necessarily members of the old elite (who still concentrated on the cities in the west), but who were from new social groups. The survival of the university, especially in the years between 1855 and 1875, was due to two factors. For one, the number of students from the province of Groningen increased. Whereas the university had traditionally been focused on city dwellers, during the nineteenth century it also attracted rural inhabitants and the province overtook the city as the primary recruiting grounds for students. The second reason is that the upper classes of Groningen started being based in the west. This sounds counter-intuitive, but they retained strong ties to their home and they actively defended local interests, a fact which kept the university afloat in the sixties and seventies, when only about thirty new students entered annually.

The Second Academy Building, 1850

The main university building, housed in a former monastery, had been adapted and rebuilt at various times since 1614. By the nineteenth century it was hopelessly inadequate to its task. In 1840 the rector lamented that nowhere 'would one encounter such a poorly-equipped cowshed'. The long lobbied for government funds to replace the building allowed the university to demolish it in 1846. In its place rose a neoclassical edifice with a facade of Ionic columns, designed by the assistant city architect J.F. Scheepers, which was officially opened in 1850. The oration delivered by the rector and professor of law, Jacob Herman Philipse, to mark the occasion was given in Dutch rather than the usual Latin. The building was refurbished in the 1870s and became even more grand.

The Acts of 1863 & 1876

At the instigation of J.R. Thorbecke, the minister of internal affairs, the Secondary Education Act of 1863 established state schools for higher citizens (*rijks hogere-burgerscholen* or HBS) which offered three-year and five-year programmes. Groningen's first HBS with a five-year programme was established in 1864. Although not originally intended as a route to university, HBS students could go on to further study if they passed the required national exams or had special dispensations to do so. The success of such students was most clearly demonstrated by the six Nobel Prize winners who had been in

Academy Building of 1850

the HBS system before 1914.

The Higher Education Act of 1876 gave the university its modern name, *Rijksuniversiteit Groningen* (literally 'State University of Groningen' but usually translated as 'University of Groningen'). The act regulated which subjects were to be taught at Dutch universities and laid down that classes should be given in the vernacular, but that the academic calendar should continue to be in Latin. It also contained rules to which programmes had to adhere: syllabuses were to be determined in June, they were to specify whether a course would take half a year or longer and the number of hours a week in which it would be taught. A minor regulation from 1876 which is still visible today is the instruction that professors should wear black togas on formal occasions. This uniformity makes a Dutch academic procession a good deal more sober than the multicoloured display of countries where participants wear the gowns of the institutions from which they graduated.

At a more general level, the act also provided a vision for higher education whose role was articulated in terms of the 'civilisation' of young men (a demanding task indeed). This showed the influence of the German notion of *Bildung*. However, the act stipulated that students should be prepared for specific professions and it called for more specialisation than before. It also included an emphasis on science and on research. To achieve all of this, more investment had to be made in facilities and salaries were increased. One result was parliamentary muttering at the unnecessary expense.

The 1876 act prescribed that at least one university must offer classes in French, English, and German. At Groningen, this led to the appointment of Barend Sijmons (1853–1935) as the first professor of modern languages. It also resulted in the arrival of the study of English at the university thus founding the oldest English department in the Netherlands in 1886. Prior to the nineteenth century it was not possible to study English in a regular institutional setting, much less at a university. Whoever wanted to learn the language had to do so through self-study with the help of textbooks. Even so, by 1840 a fair number of people were reported to have been able to read and write English quite well, but their oral proficiency was often deficient. Later, it became possible to learn English in secondary schools and in 1863 it even became compulsory for pupils in higher secondary education to study it. Before then, and perhaps even some time afterwards, the Dutch elite had little knowledge of the English language. Those who learnt it usually did so for commercial purposes, and, as such, the middle classes had the most to gain from it.

Social Change

The university had fulfilled a social role that was conservative in that it had primarily trained students for functions that would keep the fibre of traditional society intact. In the first half of the nineteenth century these were determined by the boundaries of a class-based society in which the formation of a state had begun but was far from complete. The University of Groningen had primarily educated local nobility who were expected to play a constructive part in a monarchical regime. The balance of power in the period was in the hands of patricians and the learned class was politically weak. Nationally, this began to change over time and the university followed this trend.

In the transition from catering for the ruling caste to that of preparing a strategic elite the university had to justify its position by showing its utility to society rather than by appealing to privileges based on titles and birth rights. An academic degree and an academic culture became important instruments in forging civil society. Higher education contributed to realising the principles of the Enlightenment. By 1890 the social profile of the university had changed considerably. New social classes attended it and now the sons of farmers and teachers were to the fore. This social democratisation of the university facilitated a rise in student numbers and helped, for a time, to secure its future.

Star Gazing: J.C. Kapteyn

Jacobus Cornelius Kapteyn (1851–1922) was born in Barneveld, the ninth of fifteen children. He studied mathematics and physics at Utrecht where he was awarded his doctorate. He took up a position at the observatory in Leiden that launched his career in astronomy. In 1878, while only twenty-seven, he became the first professor of astronomy and theoretical mechanics at Groningen, a position he held until 1921. His expertise was the movement of stars and what this suggested about the structure of the universe. He was involved in collecting observational data that greatly assisted others working in different areas of astronomy. This was remarkable since the university had no observatory. Kapteyn got around this fundamental problem by entering into suitable collaborations that allowed him to publish the positions of more than 450,000 stars in the southern hemisphere. When Word War I broke out, this man who was involved in numerous and productive international academic links was appalled. When it ended, he resigned from the Royal Dutch Academy after it decided to join an international research council which excluded Germany.

In 1965 the Groningen's Kapteyn Observatory was opened at Roden, in Drenthe. Although this was closed in 1996, Kapteyn's name was given to the Astronomical Institute which houses Groningen's Department of Astronomy. In 2008 the Blaauw Observatory was opened. It is equipped with a 40cm refractor telescope (one of the largest in the Netherlands). Students of astronomy keep up Kapteyn's international tradition by training for part of their time with a telescope in the Canary Islands.

STUDENT SOCIETIES

The roots of Groningen's student societies gathered around the Dutch-language *Journal for the History and Critical Appraisal of Philosophy* founded by Theodorus van Swinderen (1784–1851), a man who would go on to become a university professor in 1799. This group was primarily led by younger graduates, often those who had only just finished their studies. In 1810 the *Magazijn* fused with that of another group, the Society

Student in uniform, c.1830

for Physics. Van Swinderen was also a founder of *Veritas et Officium* which focused on the philosophy of Kant, stressing the elevation of mind, heart and taste. Van Swinderen firmly believed that student societies were of paramount importance for forming character.

February 1815 saw the establishment of Groningen's oldest surviving student association *Vindicat atque Polit* ('Preserve and refine'). Vindicat was the continuation of an eighteenth-century trend in which an increasingly strong *esprit de corps* showed itself in participation in academic events that included student representatives. At its founding, Vindicat was essentially a student senate concerned with protecting the rights and interests of the students, keeping peace amongst them and promoting 'civility'. The society organised the student community for celebrations and for funerals. Initially, the former were limited to two: when a new rector was inaugurated for the university and when one was inaugurated for Vindicat itself. When a member died, Vindicat was responsible for arranging the manner the students mourned. It also published an *Almanak*.

Today, Vindicat has about 2,000 students and it runs social and sports events. In addition to its prominent headquarters on the Grote Markt it owns 200 houses in the city. It has survived various break-away groups and the destruction of the society's building at the end of the Second World War. The storms it is currently weathering include controversy about the rowdiness of its carousing, and more seriously, violence in the initiation of new members, the university's grant of €33,000 to pay its board members has been suspended. As a consequence, 'Civilising' must again be high on its agenda.

The Third Academy Building, 1909

The outside of the Academy Building was being repainted in August 1906 when a fire broke out that was impossible to control. Some braved the flames to save the archives, professors' portraits and any other precious things that came to hand, but the structure was gutted. Its replacement, the Academy Building, which was designed by the state architect J.A. Vrijman, opened in 1909. Its northern Renaissance style contrasted sharply with the previous edifice: instead it hearkened back to the era in which the university had been founded.

The exterior decoration bears a message for passers by. At the apex of the facade over the front stairs can be seen the lion of the Netherlands below which is a statue of Minerva, goddess of wisdom, standing over the crest of the university. Below the crest stand allegorical statues of Knowledge and History who are accompanied by Prudence and Mathematics on the top of the left and right-hand gables. The carillon's bells in the tower at the west end help staff and students keep the time by sounding every half hour. A computer works the hammers most of the time, but on Tuesday mornings and on special occasions it gives way to the university's carilloneur, Auke de Boer, who has held his post since 1996.

The Heymanszaal

On the ground floor of the Academy Building at its east end is *De Heymanszaal* (The Heymans' Room) which is named after Gerard Heymans (1857–1930), professor of

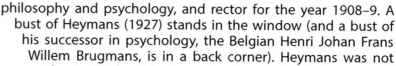

philosophy and psychology, and rector for the year 1908–9. A bust of Heymans (1927) stands in the window (and a bust of his successor in psychology, the Belgian Henri Johan Frans Willem Brugmans, is in a back corner). Heymans was not enthusiastic about having a bust made in his honour and was only mollified by the knowledge that he would be giving the sculptor, W.J. Valk, employment.

Heymans studied in Leiden where he earned doctorates in legal philosophy and economics. He was appointed professor at Groningen in 1890, a post he held until 1925. He was the founder of Dutch experimental psychology having successfully argued that the university should invest in the requisite equipment. He had a laboratory in a room adjoining the lecture hall that now bears his name. Heymans researched perception and optical illusions, character types and parapsychology (the study of the paranormal). As a philosopher, he held to psychic monism, the assertion that ultimate reality is psychological.

Heymans pioneered education as a university subject and lectured teachers on psychology, laying the foundation for the Netherlands' first education programme (established at Groningen in 1927). Dutch education was changing significantly at the time. In 1901 primary schooling became compulsory. In the late nineteenth and early twentieth century the 'school conflict' over the question of financing private (i.e. religious) schools raged and this was only settled in 1917 with a law which made access to government funds equal for both public and private institutions.

Although a shy man, Heymans did not shun public affairs. In 1898 he repudiated his Legion of Honour medal because of the anti-Semitic miscarriage of justice that was the Dreyfus Affair. He regarded war as senseless, a point he argued in his pamphlet *To the Citizens of the Belligerent States* (1914), a publication of the Dutch branch of the European Federation in the committee of which he served alongside Aletta Jacobs. Admitting that no-one (including himself) was truly neutral in the matter, Heymans addressed his readers, reminding them of ubiquitous propaganda: 'Do you think it at all likely that in a so long previously prepared and so complicated a conflict as the one under discussion, justice and truth should have ranked themselves wholly on the one side, and their opposites on the other?' His psychological training was visible in his focus on people's natural biases and his optimism in believing that these could be partially put aside. He was consistent after the war and, alongside his colleague J.C. Kapteyn, he opposed the exclusion of Germany from the International Research Council.

SENATE ROOM PORTRAITS

Amongst the treasures rescued from the fire of 1906 were the portraits of past professors. These include four paintings from 1618 (Ubbo Emmius, Nicolaas Mulerius, Cornelius Pijnacker and Hermann Ravensberger); but, alas, there was no continuous tradition of portraits and many professors are absent from the collection. Over a hundred and fifty professors can, however, be found in the Senate Room where they line its walls. It is fitting that they are mute as the Academic Senate has been abolished and the room is now used for ceremonial occasions. There are only three women in the portraits, Jantina Tammes (1871–1947), who had the chair of botany, Elizabeth Visser (see page 86), and Wilhelmina Bladergroen (1908–83), who worked in education and child psychology. Bladergroen had run a private school that she started for special needs pupils and having concealed Jewish children amongst her boarders during the occupation, she was briefly imprisoned. New portraits are being added to the collection and these, which include several more women, are dispersed in the faculty rooms of the Academy Building.

CHAPTER EIGHT

WOMEN

THE first woman who attended lectures at a Dutch university was the Cologne-born writer and artist Anna Maria van Schurman (1607–78). She was considered a prodigy of learning and respect for her is attested by her invitation to write Latin poems to celebrate the founding of the University of Utrecht. She was allowed to be an auditor at lectures there on condition that she was separated from the rest of the students and accompanied by servants. She wrote in defence of women's studying, although this was a qualified defence and one she wished to retract to some extent later in her life.

Two centuries later, the Secondary Education Act of 1863 made it possible for local authorities to establish secondary schools for girls with various educational programmes. In practical terms this was more of a landmark for women's education than the special case of van Schurman. The state did not consider the education of girls of such importance that it wanted to manage their schools itself. The first of these was established in Haarlem in 1867, and of the six that followed in 1871 and 1872, one was established in the city of Groningen. Although the arrival of secondary schools for girls theoretically opened up more educational possibilities, the goal of such institutions remained the formation of well-mannered ladies. Preparing them for a profession or academic study was out of the question.

ALETTA JACOBS

The first female student of the university, Aletta Jacobs, remains one of its best known women alumni. She was the eight of twelve children born into a Jewish family in Sappemeer, a small village in the province of Groningen, on 9 February 1854. As a child she did not realise that girls from her social background were destined to go on to other jobs than boys would. As she observed:

> At the age of six, I solemnly announced that I wanted to be a doctor, just like Dad and Julius [her eldest brother, whom she worshipped]. At that point I never imagined that this would be a particularly difficult choice for a girl. Why should it have been? At home the boys and the girls were treated the same: we went to the same school, attended the same classes ... Father never tried to dissuade me and even actively encouraged me.

Her progressive family provided more than inspiration, it also gave practical support to her and her sisters. Of these, Frederika was the first girl to pass Dutch secondary school exams in mathematics and book keeping, and Charlotte became a student at Groningen, as well as the first qualified female pharmacist.

Girls' secondary schools taught subjects such as French, needlework and etiquette. After Jacobs left primary school in 1867, she was unable to take advantage of the possibilities of the Secondary Education Act locally. However, her relations did not reject her wish to continue studying. In the absence of a better alternative, Jacobs began at

◀ *Bust by Theresia van der Plant, unveiled in 1990 on the day the first Aletta Jacobs Prize was awarded* a traditional ladies' school, but she only lasted fourteen days there. She recalled that 'I felt I was getting dumber there by the moment.' It was decided instead that she would help her mother with the household during the day and that she would be taught French and German in the evening. Since it soon became clear that Jacobs was bored by domestic chores, in 1868 she started working at for a ladies' tailor in her village. The young Aletta had a despairing realisation: 'I can never amount to anything because I am a girl.' After that, her father Abraham, and her brother Julius started teaching her Latin and Greek, possibly because they wanted to prepare her for a medical study in some way.

Dr Levi Ali Cohen, the state medical inspector in Groningen, was a friend of the Jacobs family and it was he who informed them that a girl had participated in an exam for apprentice pharmacists in 1869. He suggested that Jacobs might do the same. Anna Maria Margaretha Storm-van der Chijs (1814–95), a well-known advocate for improved education for girls, can be credited with persuading the national medical inspector to allow girls to take this test. The Physicians' Act of 1865 laid down that the exam would consist of basic language questions about Dutch and Latin as well as mathematics. Moreover, a candidate had to prove that he or she had the knowledge and skill necessary to be able to deal with prescriptions. Jacobs's home-schooled knowledge of Latin proved sufficient. She had also started working for her brother Sam, a pharmacist in Arnhem, to prepare herself for the other parts of the exam. In July 1865 she passed it (in Amsterdam) when she was sixteen years of age.

Jacobs rejected advice to continue studying to become a pharmacist because she still planned to become a physician. To do so, she had to take a university entrance exam which she could prepare for by private schooling. This would be time-consuming and it would also be uncertain whether she would in fact eventually be granted permission to enter a university. In 1868, Abraham Jacobs decided to ask the director of the HBS if his daughter could attend courses in its three-year programme. Dr Jacobs knew the HBS because two of his sons already attended there. Apparently, the director did not object to a girl's presence. The fact that some pupils only attended a selection of courses was not uncommon.

ADMISSION

Another friend of the Jacobs family, Samuel Sigmund Rosenstein, a Groningen professor of medicine, informed them that the son of a colleague who had passed the exam for apprentice pharmacists and who wanted to study mathematics and physics, had been given a dispensation from the admission exam for Groningen. Jacobs could be eligible to make use of the same regulation. She duly wrote a letter to the Dutch senate and the house of representatives on 22 March 1871. On behalf of the government, the prime minister, Johan Rudolph Thorbecke, responded to Dr Jacobs (rather than to his daughter). She might attend the university; but, paradoxically, she would have to return at a future date to the minister to receive permission to have the admission exam dispensed. On 20 April 1871 Jacobs was registered as a student at Groningen and was introduced to the professors by her brother Julius. Neither in the meetings of the Academic Senate nor in those of the Faculty of Medicine had Jacobs's entry been a topic of debate.

J.R.Thorbecke

The Future of Women

At the time that Groningen was admitting its first female student, liberals in particular had begun to look differently on the questions of the education of women and on women in the workplace, because of the example of America and arguments such as those set forth in John Stuart Mill's *The Subjection of Women* (1869). Reports from America where boys and girls attended primary education, secondary education and university together were debated in Dutch newspapers and pamphlets. Mill's book was translated into Dutch a year after it appeared in English. He argued that there is no reason why women should be raised differently, or why some professions should be inaccessible to them. It was greatly admired in liberal circles. Two Groningen professors, Bernhard van der Wijck (1836–1925) and a lawyer, B.D.H. Tellegen (1823–85), decided to write pamphlets in support of further education for women. Jacobs mentions reading both Mill and Tellegen's *De Toekomst der Vrouw* (The Future of Women), the latter of which 'affected me deeply'. In addition, it is likely that she read Van der Wijck's *De Opvoeding der Vrouw* (The Education of Women) as she owned a copy of it.

It should be borne in mind that van der Wijck and Tellegen referred to girls and women from better-off classes in their writing. They were not concerned with working-class families. Van der Wijck advanced several arguments. Firstly, he foresaw that women would start to feel bored in marriage because jobs such as spinning and weaving would be taken over by machinery. Secondly, he believed that well-educated and intelligent women would be able to raise better sons than those who 'are sick and weak of brain, slow, prejudiced, and nervous as a result of their meaningless past'. An educated wife might influence her husband in a positive manner. According to van der Wijck, an uneducated woman only seeks to benefit her own family. Education was the tool 'to open the woman's eyes to the greater good of humanity'.

Tellegen was concerned about the fates of poorly educated women who married late in life, if at all. Moreover, he believed married women should be allowed to advance in society. He claimed that opponents of emancipation were wrong in saying that in the workforce women lost their femininity and that the experience made them ill-suited to be wives. It is striking that both professors pleaded for the better education of women but did not provide any recommendation as to how this goal could be practically realised. For example, they did not state that secondary education, HBS, and university should be accessible to them.

It is evident that the liberals in Groningen did not entirely agree with Mill's ideas. Even Dr A. Johannes Vitringa, who wrote the prologue for the Dutch translation of Mill's book, believed that its author was too radical. Vitringa crystallized the difference between men and women: 'The man represents the higher order of reason by eminence, the woman that of feeling and the emotional life'. Given the hesitant response to Mill, it is even more remarkable that Prof. Rosenstein informed Jacobs of the possibility of a woman attending the university. However, once Jacobs became a student, the professors accepted her readily although she had to attend anatomy classes separately from male students. Moreover, she was allocated a room of her own in which she could rest during the fifteen-minute break between lectures. She did not put up with the special

B.D.H. Tellegen

treatment for long. She once ironically stated to her 'sweet and patient mentor' that she did not wish to be regarded as exceptional.

REACTIONS

The students in Groningen seem to have reacted positively to the arrival of their first female peer. At least, Jacobs almost never mentions negative responses from them. Shortly after her registration the national student magazine published the following observation:

> *Miss Jacobs has started classes in medicine and philosophy. The professors as well as the students have given her a warm welcome. Since a woman studying does not appear to give rise to objections, we do not hesitate to direct women's attention to subjects which are not aimed at their acquiring a function, but at greater literary development.*

Did such ladies actually appear? It is possible that women attended classes without registering officially. There may have been female attendees in 1870–1, but official university accounts only mention one in those years.

A student at Leiden objected to Jacobs's studying in an article he published. This 'Theodoor' was well informed, and he pointed out that Jacobs had been given an exemption from the admission exam. He scornfully enquired what other exemptions she would apply for. He also asked if women who intended to be doctors should learn about medicine in some other department rather than having professors teach mixed sex classes. Theodoor advised the students in Groningen to make life hard for her to precipitate her leaving. A Groningen contributer to what had become a debate and who signed himself as 'O.' (Heike Kamerlingh Onnes), opposed Theodoor's views. Of her admission exam he wrote: 'since she is the first [woman at the university], she has suffered a lack of proper education in the past. When there is need for better education, women will automatically be in the position to prepare themselves thoroughly for life in the academy'. In a somewhat high-flown manner he added:

> *We are grateful for Miss Jacobs's confidence in us. She has made it clear that she knew that there were no Theodoors at our university. The fact that we have not betrayed her trust is something we can be proud of at Groningen. That's why your [Theodoor's] words offend us and I must take up the gauntlet on her behalf.*

It was not only a Leiden student who objected. The national press opposed Jacobs and the religious press suggested that her strategy was to get sexual access to young university men! In the consequent furore, her brother Sam told their father that Jacobs would be better off doing the washing than bringing notoriety on their family. Another brother, Johan, who was in the army, was teased by his fellows to such an extent that he swore to have nothing further to do with his sibling.

NOBEL DEFENDER

Born near the A-Kerk in Groningen city centre into a well-to-do family, Heike Kamerlingh Onnes (1853–1926) studied at one of the newly-founded HBS before registering at the University of Groningen in 1870. His defence of Jacobs's presence at the university was in keeping with his belief that a *gymnasium* education should not be necessary for entry into a university, especially for the study of science. (On the other hand, he stated that a *gymnasium* formation was absolutely required for the humanities and very practical for theology and law.) Having graduated, Kamerlingh Onnes studied briefly at Heidelberg where he was taught chemistry by Robert Bunsen (the inventory of the burner). Back in Groningen he wrote his dissertation on Foucault's pendulum (which showed that the earth rotated on its axis) and was conferred with the degree of doctor, *magna cum laude*, in 1879. He went on to teach at Delft and at Leiden, where he was professor of experimental physics. In 1913 he was awarded the Nobel Prize for his work on the properties of matter at low temperatures. The Heike Kamerlingh Onnes chair is currently held by Bart van Wees of the Zernike Institute for Advanced Materials, a recipient of the Spinoza Prize.

THE PRIME MINISTER & THE KING

Dr Jacobs again asked the prime minister for the required exemption from the admission exam a few months after Aletta's registration. In June 1891 he wrote that his daughter 'had been registered as a student in medicine by the *rector magnificus* on 20 April and has uninterruptedly attended classes in mathematics and physics in addition to logic' and that 'neither the professors, nor the students have objected, but instead she has received the most praiseworthy reception'. Thorbecke, however, while he would not reject the possibility, refused to give the required dispensation. The situation became critical a year later when rumour had it that the prime minister was suffering from a serious illness. It was questionable whether his successor would even consider the possibility of a women attending university, so Dr Jacobs decided to write a third time with the information that his daughter had passed her chemistry and mathematics exams and all that all that was left in the propaedeutic phase of her degree were her exams in botany and physics, after which she would require a dispensation from the admission exam if she were to continue her study.

Thorbecke requested royal permission and in a letter of 30 May 1872 he 'granted, on behalf of the king, that Ms A.H. Jacobs from Sappemeer, in the academic degree of medicine is exempted from the so-called admission exam'. It was one of his last official actions as he died on 4 June. His permission meant that women could now in fact study at a university.

DESPAIR & DISSERTATION

In her memoirs Jacobs describes how difficult she found the time preceding the propaedeutic exams. This was partly due to personal circumstances as she was not sure whether she had made the right decision in going to university. At times, the subjects she was studying did not appeal to her. For instance, she considered anatomy 'unbelievably dull' and she always found it difficult to experiment on live animals. The propaedeutic exams took place in March and April 1874 and she passed them easily. She spent the following summer months in Lochem, a small city in Gelderland (south-east of Groningen) where her brother Julius had settled. When she came back to Groningen in September she boarded at the home of a carpenter named Fockens at Turftorenstraat 23 where her brother had lived a few years earlier.

The preparations for Jacobs's *doctoraalexamen* were hampered by malaria in the spring of 1876, a disease she had suffered from in the past. She was diagnosed with tuberculosis and this drove her to despair. Determined to end her life, she had reached her father's medical cabinet only to discover the he was waiting for her to try just that. A second opinion revealed that she was not as ill as she had been told and she returned to her studies. Despite her bad health she passed her *doctoraalexamen* in September 1876. After this, she had to get ready for the state medical exam, in those days one that was hosted in a rotation of the country's universities. In 1877, it was in Amsterdam, so Jacobs went there to meet the professors who were on the exam board. In her memoirs she mentions an additional reason to leave Groningen: after her *doctoraalexamen* she had stayed at Julius' place in Lochem and had found that the change of air had had a positive effect on her health. She registered in Amsterdam in 1876 and passed the first part of the medical exam in April the following year even though she

Jacobs's Desk

was unwell again. After this she had to be taken to hospital where the consulting physician diagnosed her with typhus. She was sick for nearly half a year and only returned to Amsterdam after the winter holidays so that she finally graduated in 1878 in Utrecht (the location of that year's test). She could now practice as a GP, but she went on to take her doctoral degree in medicine.

Jacobs prepared for the defence of her thesis back home in Sappemeer where she also assisted her father in his medical practice. For quite some time it looked as if she would never achieve her goal since he fell seriously ill in the summer of 1878. Friends in Amsterdam persuaded her to keep writing her dissertation. With *On the Localisation of Physiological and Pathological Phenomena in the Cerebrum* she graduated on 8 March 1879. A total of eight Dutch women studied medicine before 1900. (One of them, Cornelia de Lange, would become the first female professor in the Netherlands in 1927.)

Later Life, 1879–1929

After receiving her degree Jacobs led a very varied life. She left for Amsterdam and then travelled to London. Later, in 1911–12 she went much further and visited parts of Africa and Asia. Back in Amsterdam she practiced medicine. In 1892 she married Carel Gerritsen and they had one child who survived only briefly. After the death of her brother Julius, the couple adopted his son, Charles, with whom Jacobs ultimately had a troubled relationship. On top of this he may have given her the financial advice that ended in her bankruptcy in 1922, after which she was supported by the generosity of her friends.

Jacobs was an active pacifist (despite having three brothers in the military). However, the greatest part of her time was given over to the struggle for the rights of women to which end she translated two important feminist books into Dutch, Charlotte Perkins Gilman's *Women and Economics: A Study of the Economic Relation Between Men and Women as a Factor in Social Evolution* (1898) and Olive Schreiner's *Women and Labour* (1911). She was an advocate and provider of birth control, and although as an atheist ('Damned religion gives so many people kinks in the brain') she had no religious scruples about this, she entertained some doubts about the effect contraception might have on population levels and the spread of adultery.

She engaged with the medical needs of prostitutes, a group of women largely ignored by contemporary charity. This care had it roots in her training days at the Groningen hospital where she was appalled at the suffering of a woman with syphilis who was described by the obfuscating Latin term *meretrix* (whore). When, in later life, a distinguished professor explained that men's health required the expression of their sexual urges and that society had to make provision for this, an unimpressed Jacobs observed tartly that 'you'd better make sure that your daughters are made available for this purpose.' That was the end of the discussion.

Above all, Jacobs was intensely involved in the debates about women's suffrage (Dutch women received the right to vote in 1919, two years after universal male suffrage). Her public career brought her to several continents and she held discussions with President Woodrow Wilson, Pope Benedict XV and Sir Edward Grey, the British foreign secretary.

The university that had admitted the first female student did not show much support for women's emancipation. One rector, the professor of English language and literature, Johan Hendrik Kern (1867–1933), remarked in a speech in 1913 that 'the customs of the English suffragettes have fortunately not reached our country, and the student girls have better things to do than worry about the right to vote'. Nevertheless, the university did not forget Dr Jacobs. On the fiftieth anniversary of her *doctoraalexamen* the Groningen Women's Student Association sent her a telegram of congratulations and

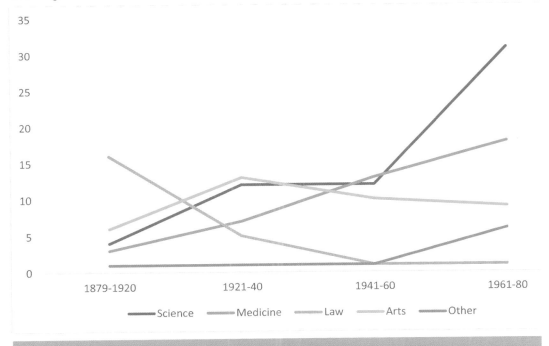

Number of women conferred with doctorates per faculty, 1879–1980

the rector and senate addressed a letter to her in which they observed: 'that a woman showed such courage to choose and complete an academic study back then in the Faculty of Medicine is an event that makes this memory even more vivid'. When Jacobs died a few months later, on 10 August 1929, a funeral wreath was sent by the university. Since then, she has been an emblem of women's rights, and to mark her birthday in 2017 she was the Google Doodle. Her autobiography, *Memories,* was published in an English translation in 1996.

The Early Debate: Women in Science

On 12 June 1872, the front page of the *Groninger Courant* reported that in Zurich a woman had became a physician and that the professors did not like the influx of female students. According to them, passing an exam did not necessarily mean that women would become good medical practitioners. One noted that 'the most important point, especially in medical science, is its practical application. The ladies have yet to prove that their knowledge benefits society'. Newspaper reports such as these are an indication of the way people abroad and in the Netherlands thought about female students. The debate on this subject

Jantine Tammes (1931)

intensified with the arrival of the first wave of feminism. In 1897 a journalist, Arthur Kirchhoff, published a book based on his interviews with several German professors on the topic of the suitability of women as university students. Most were negative. Others thought women were only fit for studies other than their own. Two Dutch academics, the botanist Melchior Treub and Cornelis Winkler, a professor of psychiatry, were invited by the Women's Interest Society to debate 'Women and Education'. Treub did not see any reason why women were less capable of studying than men. He made short work of Kirchhoff's book, and listed the scientific jobs that had been performed by women. Like Van der Wijck and Tellegen he noted that women of 'the civilised class' were educated for no more than their possible marriages, although quarter of them remained single. The pointless existence to which unmarried women were doomed troubled Treub. Why should women with the capacity to do so not study at an academic level?

Polytope model by Alicia Boole-Stott

His opponent asserted that women possessed significantly less brain capacity than men, something generally accepted at the time. According to him, women were overly emotional and suggestible which made them unsuitable for study. Moreover, he feared that women who studied might choose not to have children. A physician might be a profession for which women were suitable 'since medicine requires the least intellectual knowledge, while without affective ability no medical practitioner can do the job'. However, women could not become physicians 'in the full sense of the word' as they were incapable of the physical demands of practices in the countryside and they were not competent for surgical work.

Despite such arguments, it was clear that the gates had been opened for women in academe. In 1911, Jantine Tammes (1871–1947) became the first woman to be conferred with an honorary doctorate (in botany and zoology) by Groningen, where she became its first female professor in 1919 (the second one in the country). She had been a founder, in 1912, of Magna Pete, the oldest sorority in the Netherlands. In 1914 the university conferred an honorary doctorate on Alicia Boole-Stott (1860–1940), an Irish geometer who had worked with Groningen's professor of mathematics, Pieter Hendrik Schoute (1846–1913). This awareness of women's contribution to medicine and science continued, albeit as a trickle rather than a torrent. In the celebration of the 365th anniversary of the university in 1979 another female scientist was conferred with an honorary doctorate, Edith Bülbring (1903–90), Oxford's professor of pharmacology, who had trained as a physician. The present dean of the medical faculty is Marian Joëls, a professor of neurobiology who has previously held chairs at Amsterdam and Utrecht.

The Faculty of Arts

Hermine Christine Hélène Moquette (1869–1945) was born in Sluis, in the south of the Netherlands on 25 April 1869. In 1895, having studied Dutch literature, she became the second woman to graduate in Groningen. She went on to be an assistant archivist in Rotterdam and was accepted into the Association of Archivists of the Netherlands. Even though she replaced the archivist when he fell ill in 1904, and had a permanent contract, she was passed over for promotion; instead, an external male applicant, was given the position. It is impossible to say now who the superior candidate was, but

Moquette's may have been an early case of her profession's glass ceiling. She retired in 1929.

Groningen was the first Dutch university to appoint a female lecturer: in 1907 Maria Elise Loke (1870–1916), who had received her doctorate at Toulouse, was hired to teach French. The Paris edition of *The New York Herald* observed that 'the professional body of the Dutch universities has ceased to be exclusively masculine'. She is commemorated by the room named after her in the Harmony Building. Almost a decade later, in 1916, Dr Maria Elisabeth de Meester became the first woman to be recognised as a *privatdozentin* in English. She had received her PhD from Heidelberg in 1915 with a thesis on *Oriental Influences in the English Literature of the Nineteenth Century*. The university did not pay private lecturers (they earned their fees from students), so de Meester also had to work in a secondary school. She left Groningen to teach in Tilburg in 1918.

The first woman to be awarded a PhD on literature in English was Jantina Henderika van Klooster, who was remarkable for several reasons. Born in Groningen, she enrolled for Dutch literature, but having spent a year in New York where her brother

Elizabeth Visser

was a professor of chemistry, she had the opportunity to study at Columbia University. Back in Groningen in 1924, she was awarded a doctorate for a thesis on Edith Wharton, who had won the Pulitzer Prize for *The Age of Innocence* (1920). Klooster moved to Amsterdam with her partner Koos Schregardus and the couple founded De Spieghel publishing house. This was closed in 1942 during the occupation when they refused to register with the German authorities. They then became members of the Dutch resistance, using their home as a safe house. Both were arrested and van Klooster died at Ravensbrück. Her brother established a fund that paid for the plaques in the Academy Building that record the members of the academic community who died during the war. It also funded scholarships for women.

On her appointment at Groningen in 1947, Elizabeth (C.E.) Visser (1908–87), a graduate of the University of Amsterdam, became the first female professor of history in the country. Her field was Ancient history, particularly that of Greece. In 1964 she was made pro-rector, one of very many institutional and voluntary obligations that she took on. She identified two types of professor, those who managed to withdraw and focus on their writing and those, like herself, who paid the price for failing to be unmoved by things around her.

The current dean of Arts, who was appointed in 2009, is Gerry (Gerrigje) Wakker (1958–) who studied at the University of Amsterdam and the École Normale Supérieure in Paris before moving with her family to Groningen. She was appointed professor of Ancient Greek linguistics in 2008. Since 2012 she has been pro-rector of the university. In recognition of her service and scholarship she was made an Officer of the Order of Orange-Nassau by a representative of the king in 2018.

Dr Jacobs's Legacy

The University of Groningen rightly celebrates changes since the time of Aletta Jacobs and her name is revered: she has a room in the University Museum, her statue guards the entrance of the Harmony Building, and her spirit has the dubious satisfaction of presiding over the strain of the thousands of students who pass through the Aletta Jacobs Hall on the Zernike Campus, the university's main exam building (one that is about to double in size). The university and the UMCG run the Aletta Jacobs School of Public Health, which has a focus on the role of social justice and well-being. Since 1990, Groningen has awarded the biannual Aletta Jacobs Prize 'to a woman with an academic background who has contributed to women's emancipation in the national or international arena'. Its winners have included several politicians, women involved in international organizations, and a diverse range of contributors to art, law, economics, and, appropriately, medicine. In 2018 the prize was given to Lilianne Ploumen, a Dutch parliamentarian who had been a minister for foreign trade. It was awarded in recognition of her service on the World Bank's Advisory Council on Gender and Development and her founding of 'She Decides', a fund to counter cuts in American family planning aid introduced by the Trump presidency.

Looking back on the debates about women and education in the nineteenth and early twentieth centuries it is easy to be dismissive of outdated beliefs about gender roles. There is a good deal less agreement about where things in the university are now, or perhaps more accurately, about where they should go in the future. Only 25% of the university's 400 full professors are female, a number that is close to a fluctuating (but improving) national average. In 2003, in partnership with the EU, Groningen began appointing Rosalind Franklin fellows as part of an internationally aimed programme to attract women with PhDs who could be put on track for a professorship (an English chemist, Franklin's work helped in the discovery of DNA). However, even though a hundred fellowships have been created, this scheme in itself can only play a small part in any gender rebalancing of senior staff and it does nothing for the promotion of existing female staff members. Broader possibilities, such as positive discrimination, are rejected by many people, both men and women (few wish to be appointed on anything other than academic merit and few wish to work under anyone but the best person). There is no feasible plan that could rectify the gender imbalance quickly and this makes it more difficult to tackle as solutions requiring long-term strategies and shifts in social attitudes can be endlessly debated, derailed or abandoned.

◄ After this book was first printed Cisca Wijmenga (1964–), Professor of Genetics, became the first woman to be appointed *Rector Magnificus* (beginning September 2019). Prof. Wijmenga's distinguished CV includes a Spinoza Prize, being named a knight of the Order of the Dutch Lion, over €45 million in grants, and membership of the Netherlands Royal Academy of Arts and Sciences and the Royal Holland Society of Sciences and Humanities. ►

CHAPTER NINE

1914-1950: WAR

THE most visible remnants of the tercentenary celebrations are now the windows in the stairwell of the Academy Building which were gifts from the city, the province and private donors. Made by the brothers Rudolf and Otto Linnemann from Frankfurt, they celebrate the history of the institution from its foundation. In the central window, *Deo Patriae Academiae*, women representing the city bear the three Academy Buildings. The central one supports the figure of Ubbo Emmius. Putti carry banners from the students' military past with the dates 1665 and 1830. (The date of 1909 on the lower pane is that of the construction of the building and not the window). The side windows show Minerva and symbols of the then five faculties.

The century of university masquerades came to an end with the one held on 1 July 1914 for the tercentenary. Re-enacting the historic events of the Peace of Westphalia (1648), the masquerade showed the declaration of the Spanish–Dutch peace. Students representing the two sides of the Thirty Years' War (1618–48) followed different routes to Groningen's city hall. There, the treaty, signed at Münster, was re-enacted, following which the participants announced general concord from a specially-built stage. An editor of the student almanac for the year wrote that 'without doubt the masquerade was a success, yet I do believe that many came to the realisation that day that the time of masquerades is at an end, that something in the spirit of the twentieth century no longer accords with such expressions of joy and energy'.

NEUTRALITY, 1914–1918

The First World War broke out only a month after the tercentenary. Although the Netherlands remained neutral, the war had profound consequences. The horrific situations on the Western front, the immense number of dead, the trenches, chemical warfare, all these deeply affected the Dutch. Sufferings were brought especially close to home by the number of Belgian refugees seeking asylum. Along with these came 1,500 members of a British Royal Navy Brigade who had accidentally strayed into the Netherlands and who, in accordance with international law, were interned in Groningen for the duration of the war in what was called 'The English Camp'.

Dutch trade was severely curtailed by the British naval blockade in the North Sea aimed at squeezing the Central Powers' access to resources

◄ *Groningen in 1945*

(the Dutch exported food to Germany and Austro-Hungary as well as to England). The Allies were just as concerned about the things which passed through neutral ports to be channelled to their enemies. As a result, the Netherlands suffered economically from the Royal Navy's actions against Germany. Near the end of the war, Dutch industrial production nearly came to a halt. The government deemed it necessary to invoke extraordinary measures and increased state intervention, which mostly involved the circulation of money and food supplies. The prime minister, P.M. Cort van der Linden, and the parliament, improvised the distribution of supplies by applying a ration card system that divided provisions equally among citizens. National solidarity facilitated great social change so that in 1917 parliament legislated for universal male franchise and for the solution to long-running disputes about the funding of schools.

The war did not pass by unnoticed at the university. The departing rector, a psychiatrist, Dirk Wiersma (1858–1940), called it a 'useless destruction of life and capital' and remarked that 'the hope of a speedy reconciliation of nations is an idle hope. On the contrary, the nations are opponents more than ever and Europe has almost entirely become a battlefield. Is it surprising that this world-shattering event forces its mark on the fate of this university?' It was hardly surprising, and the consequences were immediately visible.

On the eve of the conflict, the university staff numbered forty-three professors and five biochemistry lecturers. In the academic year 1913–14, more than 600 students enrolled. This number decreased to 470 when many were summoned for military service. A pleasant atmosphere disappeared along with the students and professors. The rector remarked, concerning what should have been the usual excitement surrounding the official opening of the academic year, 'no festive music was heard; no serenades were performed'. The mood of that day lingered. The call for students to join the army and related occupations, such as the Red Cross, was repeated during the war. A law of 31 June 1915 recruited men to join the home guard to replace those on duty with younger ones. Among them were many university students. However, lecture rooms were not completely empty due to an increasing number of students from the south of the country and the opportunity provided by the military for some mobilised students to go on study leave and spend a few months in their faculties. Most students used this time to take part in exams.

Interwar

The post-war years brought a steady increase in the numbers enrolling at the university. In part this was related to the Dutch population which grew from five million in 1899 to seven million in 1920. The university was unsure about the many enrolments. Its board wondered where they could all be accommodated and whether they would find a place in society after completing their studies. The rector, Albert Kluyver (1858–1938), linked the increasing number of students to decreasing prosperity, saying: 'One can assume that these unfortunate times make a father send his children to the university, since he does not know any other path for them'.

After the war more than sixty students applied to do literary studies and that number continued to increase. In the academic year 1925–6, it had grown to 191 students. Groningen held a monopoly on modern languages for a long time (which it only lost in 1920). After this, several professors left to teach at the University of Amsterdam and the numbers studying modern languages gradually declined: there were 163 students in 1928–9, ninety-four students in 1935–6, and thirty fewer than this in 1938–9. Nevertheless, courses in modern languages remained a prominent part of the university. Only in Groningen could people study Frisian and Old Frisian for instance. The languages that were taught in the inter-war period were: Dutch, German, Frisian, English, French, Italian, Spanish, Old Germanic, Latin, Greek, Hebrew, Arabic, and Babylonian-Assyrian. Since the faculty was so diverse, most professors had hardly any staff and they controlled the courses and structure of their departments.

In the pre-war years, the university community was probably most accurately described as 'seeking'. It was searching both for a greater internal unity and for closer integration with society at large. As the head of Vindicat stated at his inauguration in 1931: 'The times have passed when students were admired for their capacity to distance themselves from social life and when a student organisation could completely disassociate itself from the issues of society, in short, the time when people could do as they pleased'. Amongst the professors, there were also several who were politically engaged and socially active. One of the most notable was Leonard Polak (1880–1941), a philosopher with a combative personality and a great love of music. As a philosopher, he became involved in a wide range of issues: he was very active as a board member for the *Volksuniversiteit* (People's University) in Groningen. The young and idealistic royal commissioner, Johannes Linthorst Homan, also gained remarkable goodwill. He established a 'community of Groningen' to unite people from all sectors of society. His aim for more solidarity and his attempts to overcome socio-economic and political divisions were praised both by academic staff and students. Linthorst Homan introduced the idea of creating the celebratory 'Groningen Days'. As the rector, Pieter Johannes van Rhijn (1886–

Leonard Polak

1960), became a member of the advisory board of the Groningen Days the university was closely connected to the festivities. Several professors gave readings and people were welcomed into the Aula in the Academy Building. A somewhat romantic and vaguely social sense of local patriotism probably increased in popularity, because people had felt ignored by the government in the economic politics of the previous few years. Furthermore, there was a renewed interest in their Groningen identity as well as a desire to express it. The lustrum play, *Living Country*, to which many artists from Groningen contributed, captured this spirit well.

In this climate there was little sympathy for Nazi ideology because people wanted to focus on their own cultural values and growth. During the 1930s, the University Board distanced itself from official contacts with German universities; thus, none of the members wanted to represent the senate at the celebration of 550 years of the University of Heidelberg. The rector commented that 'such a gathering, in which so many scholars were excluded by the Germans, seemed unnecessary'.

HANDYMAN: FRITZ ZERNIKE

Fritz Zernike (1888–1966) had studied chemistry in his native city, Amsterdam, before moving to Groningen to become an assistant to the astronomer J.C. Kapteyn. During this period, he focused on optics rather than astronomy. In 1915 he became a lecturer in mathematical science at Groningen and five years later he was made a professor. His journey through many different sciences illustrates his versatility. He is often referred to as an all-round physicist: he knew how to combine accurate theoretical insights with a large technical virtuosity, evidence for which was provided by the improved galvanometer he invented in 1921.

Zernike was no organiser or team member; he mostly worked alone in his room. Apart from his lectures, he hardly interfered with the policies of the institution. Above all, he was known as a handyman who conducted the most amazing experiments with the simplest devices. Technicians frequently asked for his advice. There is a popular anecdote about the time when he and a number of others were stuck in a Parisian lift Zernike quickly figured out how the elevator worked and within minutes got it started again. He was not the most organised handyman: the chaos of screws, wires and bottles in his room often drove his co-workers to desperation. Nevertheless, he was always

able to find everything himself. Whenever something went missing, the chances were that Zernike had it. He preferred working at night and he would simply take whatever equipment he needed, much to the frustration of others.

The most important area of Zernike's research was optics. His best-known invention was the phase contrast microscope. This allowed the study of transparent materials with different refractive indices. Up until then, living cells could only be studied by staining the cells with colour, a process that damaged or killed them. In the 1930s, Zernike travelled by motorbike to Jena in Germany to visit the famous Zeiss company to discuss production of the microscope. Zeiss claimed not to be interested. After the Second World War, tapes were found in Jena which showed that Zeiss had secretly been working on the idea. Among the recordings were the first moving images of cell division. Zernike was awarded the Nobel Prize for Physics for his phase contrast microscope in 1953.

R.W. Zandvoort & The Anglo-American Institute

In 1937, Prof. R.W. Zandvoort inaugurated the Anglo-American Institute. Among the people who were present at the opening were the royal commissioner, the mayor of Groningen, the rector (Fritz Zernike), several professors, representatives of student societies and the Groningen board of the English Association. In his opening speech, Zandvoort clarified the intentions and goals of the Institute. Firstly, he deemed it important that people interested in English were given the opportunity to meet others in their field, from the Netherlands as well as from abroad. In this way they could share their ideas and be instructed by professional speakers, not just about English, but also about subjects that were related to the study of the English language.

The desire of students of English to study abroad for a period was fulfilled by the Anglo-American Institute. In theory, this had always been possible, but financial limitations had often put a stop to it. Zandvoort believed that a long-term stay abroad was one of the most important components in the study of a modern philologist and that lectures by prominent foreign English expert could have positive results. The Institute provided assistance to students from whom the most successful outcomes could be expected. It was open to alumni because they were given free access to lectures which served as kinds of continuation courses. According to Zandvoort, the Institute was called 'Anglo-American' rather than merely British or English, because the language and culture of the US demanded consideration. The new body was funded by the British Council and the Rockefeller Foundation. American culture had been a neglected topic in Dutch universities and the first steps in its exploration were due in a large part to Groningen. In 1952 an America Institute was founded in Amsterdam. Zandvoort became the first president of the European Association of American Studies in 1954. Groningen appointed a junior professor with an expertise in American literature in 1955: Eric Mottram (1924–95) commented on the 'almost universal academic suspicion and ironic disdain of American Studies' in the Netherlands. Zandvoort's department was an exception. One of the long-term results was the establishing of Groningen's Department of American Studies (the only one in the Netherlands) which was founded by F. L. van Holthoon. Its first chair, Wil Verhoeven (1958–), a graduate of the English Department, gave his inaugural lecture in 2003.

To return to Zandvoort, a man of extraordinary energy and organizational ability: Reinard Willem Zandvoort (1894–1990) was born in Averhoorn in the province of North Holland. He studied at a HBS before attending the University of Groningen. As part of his studies he taught for a time in a school in England. Having received his teaching diploma from the University of Amsterdam he worked at the HBS in Nijmegen. He continued his study of English and graduated with his MA (Groningen, 1922) and PhD (Leiden, 1929). The latter was written on *The Arcadia* (c.1581–4) a prose romance by Sir Philip Sidney (who had died in the Netherlands serving with the earl of Leicester's army). In the meantime, Zandvoort had founded *English Studies* which became an international publication, and one that even managed to survive without a government subsidy. In 1937 he was appointed professor of English language and literature at Groningen where he worked until his retirement in 1964. He served as rector and pro-rector, established the International Association of University Professors of English (which met first in Oxford in 1950), and combined faculty administrative tasks with his departmental duties. His *Handbook of English Grammar* (1945), which he piloted on his own students, went through fifteen editions and was adapted for use in England, France, the US and Japan. He was made a Commander of the British Empire (CBE) by Queen Elizabeth II in 1963.

In Groningen in 1941 Zandvoort decided to lecture on *Macbeth*. He made no direct reference to the conflict going on outside university's walls:

> *War against Macbeth is being prepared in England: discontent and covert rebellion are preparing at home. Life in Scotland is becoming unbearable under Macbeth's tyrannous reign; there is no safety, there is no sincerity or freedom left. As soon as help comes from abroad, Macbeth's nobles will rise against him, to free themselves and their country from his oppression.*

War, 1940–5

On 10 May 1940, despite the promise of Hitler to Queen Wilhelmina, Germany invaded the neutral Netherlands. *Blitzkrieg* and the Luftwaffe overtook the possibility of a defensive flooding of the country and the ill-equipped Dutch army was conquered in five days. From then on, the country was ruled by an Austrian *Reichskommissar*, Arthur Seyss-Inquart. Universities were subjected to heavy pressure during the occupation: they were an important element in the policy of enforced conformity. Nazi ideology, which allowed no freedom of mind or research, was a fundamental threat to their existence. Even though it initially attempted to resist influence from the invaders and continue as normal, the university was disrupted by the crisis arising from compulsory statements of loyalty and forced employment of students in Germany.

There had been many debates about politics in the previous years. For instance, the national socialist movement (the NSB), which had been founded in 1931, was often a source of argument among students. However, these discussions mostly remained informal. The NSB received little support from academics, but no real counter movement arose. After the shock of the capitulation of the Netherlands had subsided, university life continued mostly as usual.

In the university, 'solidarity' became a popular term. This sense of solidarity was expressed, for instance, during a summer camp in Ter Apel, in which many students and staff participated. It was an informal gathering with lectures on popular culture, discussions, music and dancing. The fact that people from different student societies and none gathered together with staff in a casual setting was unique at the time. The 'ambiance of Ter Apel' remained something that was recalled in Groningen even after the war. The chemistry professor, Hilmar Johannes Backer (1882–1959), was one of the principal initiators at the heart of this gathering. He organised many other joint activities which were aimed at strengthening the community of the university.

The German authorities had great plans for the University of Groningen and actively interfered in its governance. It was to become a centre from which National Socialist ideas could be disseminated throughout the Netherlands. Groningen was considered eminently suitable for this project because of its 'popular' character and the presence of Old-Saxon and Frisian cultural elements (Germanic affiliations which, from the occupiers' perspective had been suppressed by the dominant Dutch). The invaders considered that a renewal of racial awareness might win people over to their cause. In 1940, a pro-German rector was appointed who focused on this goal. Johannes Marie Neele Kapteyn was professor of Old Germanic philology and Frisian. The departing rector, the astronomer Pieter Johannes van Rhijn, was unhappy with this and felt alarmed about handing over the rectorate.

Kapteyn (1870–1949) had had an unusual academic career. A former bookseller and schoolteacher, he was given his chair in 1924 aged 54 having received an honorary doctorate from Bonn. He served two terms as rector. A member of the NSB and a supporter of SS ideas about German culture, he eventually spent ten months in internment after the liberation of the Netherlands. Kapteyn handed over to Herman Maximilien de Burlet (1883–1957), who was rector between 1942 and 1945. Born in Rotterdam, he had received his doctorate at Zurich and was eminent enough to have been a member of the Royal Dutch Academy. He became a professor in the Faculty of Medicine in Groningen in 1931. Like Kapteyn, he was a supporter of the Nazis.

Jewish Citizens

In the city the first registration of foreign Jews began in July 1940. That November, six Jewish professors were fired. The German philosopher/sociologist, Helmuth Plessner

(1892–1985), went into hiding, in part with the help of students (after the war he was appointed professor at Groningen, returning to Germany in 1951 to a chair at Göttingen). The philosopher Leonard Polak was arrested for referring to the Germans as 'the enemy' in a letter protesting his suspension that was passed on by Rector Kapteyn to the authorities. Polak, who was a well-known Dutch intellectual and the chairman of the Dutch Atheists' Association, later died doing hard labour in the concentration camp at Sachsenhausen (his daughter, Henriëtte, a student of medicine, died in Auschwitz). The philosopher might be momentarily confused with a professor of medicine, Leonard Polak Daniels (1872–1940), who, along with his wife, committed suicide rather than face the fate planned for them.

At the university, there were rumours about a strike to protest the dismissal of the staff; however, what emerged was a formal written protest. When, a few months later, in March 1941, Jewish students were prohibited from beginning their studies, a similar protest occurred; students resisted but did not go on strike, while the university staff remained silent. In November 1941, the authorities decreed that Jews were to be denied membership of student associations. The result was that the societies voluntarily closed down to register their opposition. In the city 2,724 Jews were registered by the authorities of which more than 2,500 were killed or deported to Poland.

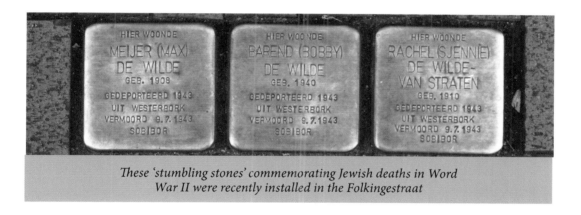

These 'stumbling stones' commemorating Jewish deaths in Word War II were recently installed in the Folkingestraat

CARRY ON

In other cities the protests by students and professors had been more vigorous, and consequently, the University of Leiden had to close in 1940. In 1941, students from Leiden were allowed to continue their studies elsewhere and many went to Groningen. This is the reason for the extraordinary growth in enrolments that year. Many Leiden students remained after the war to finish their studies.

In Groningen, more painful confrontations with the Nazi regime followed. However, the dominant opinion was that keeping the university open should be a priority. The academic staff often remained low-key to protect their institution as much as possible. The professor of mathematics, Jan van der Corput (1890–1975), attempted to unite the professors in resistance, but to little effect. At the end of 1942, tensions rose further when students stopped coming to the university because they were under threat of being called up for *Arbeitseinsatz* (mandatory work deployment) in Germany, a scheme supported by Rector de Burlet. Several students were arrested while protesting against the *Arbeitseinsatz*. By that time, the universities of Utrecht and Delft were no longer teaching. In March 1943, measures were taken to restore order: all students were to sign a statement of loyalty in which they promised not to take actions against Germany. Those who did not sign risked being sent abroad to work. The student societies immediately appealed to members not to sign and with success: only 10% did so. Van der Corput asked the senate to object to the statement of loyalty, but his plea fell on deaf ears. After further serious threats from the Germans 40% of the students eventually signed the declaration in order to keep their families safe. However, despite having signed they were still sent to Germany to work.

Classes had continued during the first years of the war. Naturally there had been disruptions such as difficult communications with colleagues abroad and shortage of supplies. The ban on radios caused problems for astronomers who needed them to receive time signals. Problems at the Astronomical Institute were exacerbated because Prof. van Rhijn was seriously ill. In the science department, Prof. Frans Maurits Jaeger (1877–1945) retired for health reasons and no successor was appointed until after 1945. Other job vacancies also remained unfilled, for instance that of the botany professor, Benedictus Hubertus Danser, who died in 1943.

Several professors acting individually attempted to help students and staff members. H.J. Backer not only organised Ter Apel, he was a contact person for students who were sent to work in Germany, collecting information, forwarding letters, and helping them find housing. The meteorologist, Prof. Dirk Coster, also helped his students to the fullest of his abilities despite his being ill. Furthermore, he sheltered Jewish fugitives and once even travelled to Berlin where he rescued Lise Meitner, a professor of physics there (who had been baptised a Christian, but who had been born into a Viennese Jewish family) by smuggling her to Groningen whence she escaped to Sweden. Another noteworthy staff member was the professor of Roman law, Johan Hendrik van Meurs (1888–1945) who resigned his chair in protest at the treatment of students. After this, he went into hiding where, refusing to participate in the black market in food, he died of malnourishment. Jan van der Corput harboured people who had gone underground. Among these was the astronomy professor, Lukas Plaut (1910–84). However, like many people in hiding, Plaut was betrayed and subsequently captured (although he worked at the Kapteyn Astronomical Institute after the war, eventually camp syndromeforced him to retire). Many stories were told about professors travelling through the province to teach students in hiding or to hold examinations. Some laboratories harboured people on the run, for instance the Geological Institute, with its many corners and staircases, offered good hiding places.

Along with the horrific circumstances of warfare itself and the increasing difficulties of food shortages, the Netherlands was deeply affected by the *hongerwinter* (hunger-winter) of 1944–5 during which 16,000–20,000 Dutch died of malnutrition, cold and disease. The *hongerwinter* was not as disastrous in Groningen as it was in the west of the country, partially due to the city's agricultural hinterland. It was common for food packages, disguised as fragile scientific instruments, to be sent from Groningen to Amsterdam or Leiden. In the winter of 1945, Groningen offered a haven for many evacuees. These were offered 'bread and a bed' inside the Harmony Building. As a result, in April 1945, a tenth of the people living in the city were refugees.

Der Clercke Cronike

Nearly all students were members of a student society. Although the aim of Vindicat to create one universal society was not realised, an umbrella organisation was created by all societies in 1933 to function as a discussion forum for students. This published *Der Clercke Cronike*, a magazine that created an opportunity for students in Groningen as well as other Dutch universities to air ideas about the blossoming sense of social accountability.

Although political controversy was not central to *Der Clercke*, after Nazi ideology reached the Netherlands it was debated from different points of view. Some were positive, some were negative, and some declared that they were not bothered (*Der Clercke* mockingly observed: 'I will not unite with the countless fools, for I am high above such things, I remain neutral on principle'). An antipathy for traditional Dutch politics even led, sometimes, to a sympathetic hearing for Anton Mussert, the leader of the NSB. The December issue of 1932 printed an article on an address Mussert gave in the Harmony Building: 'Despite the fact that his speech covered many topics which several people agreed with, overall he remained too vague and far less specific than the texts which were available in the room'. However, the emphasis on solidarity impressed the writer: 'Hopefully, national-socialism will bring unity to the chaos of the national-minded Dutch'. In June 1933, there was a very positive report of another performance by Mussert (who was executed after the war). Both these reports were very different from articles by Leo Frank, the chairman of the social-democratic student society, who warned against fascism in Italy and national-socialism in Germany.

In 1939, the main editor of *Der Clercke* wrote: 'About five years ago, there was a change in Germany, which, in my opinion, meant more than merely a change in the political sense. It was a change of spirit or rather the awakening of a dark spirit'. He was immediately reprimanded for this and retired from his post. A stream of controversy was unleashed about, among other things, the value of pacifism. When one student advocated the spiritual empowerment of pacifism, another wanted her to be locked up. The magazine commented, 'let everyone have their say so that people will realise that the Nazis are among us'. The magazine had to refrain from printing more openly political statements in the summer of 1940, but it published veiled criticism of its curtailed freedom. This went as far as a poem which ridiculed the German authorities which appeared on its front page. Such risky publications eventually led to the magazine's closure.

Der Clercke was honourably wound up when the editors refused to adhere to the censorship of the curators. The final issue was released on 14 November 1941. The two senior editors were fined 1,000 guilders and sentenced to three weeks in jail. Shortly after the war, *Der Clercke Cronike* reopened with a new edition on 19 May 1945. The front page ran an article which was directed at all students stating that the editors were re-establishing truthful communication. It praised the students who resisted during the war. *Der Clercke* remained the general student publication until 1971. It can be seen as the precursor to *UK* the current university newspaper.

A Cell with Shakespeare: Hans Gerritsen

One of the members of the editorial staff of *Der Clercke* was Johan (Hans) Gerritsen (1920–2013), an English student since 1939, and one of two board members imprisoned by the SS for three weeks in *Het Huis van Bewaring* (The House of Detention, a building that still exists on the Hereweg). Prisoners were allowed one book and Gerritsen opted for the works of Shakespeare. After his release, like other students, Gerritsen was expected to make the declaration of loyalty to the effect that he would not engage in subversive activity. Since he would not sign, he was sent to work in a Berlin machine factory (between May 1943 and April 1944), believing that if he did not do so, repercussions would be exacted on his brother. Work conditions were awful: accounts of long hours combined with fleas and scabies reached the rector's office.

After the war Gerritsen returned to his study of English. He received a grant from the

Help Holland Council to spend a year at Liverpool University. Back in Groningen in 1952 he was awarded his PhD *cum laude* for a thesis on Renaissance drama and following a stint at the Royal Library, he travelled on a Fulbright grant to the Folger Shakespeare Library. In 1964 he succeeded R.W. Zandvoort as professor of English in the department

Gerritsen's Cell

where he had been so long a student. He reluctantly retired in 1985.

As a footnote that demonstrates how things were in the university after the war it is worth mentioning that Gerritsen's employment overlapped with that of Dr Jan Verleun (1925–2011), a Conrad scholar who was a staff member between 1965 and 1986. In 1943, Verleun had joined the Waffen-SS, something he managed to conceal afterwards. However, before he died he gave an account of his life to one of his former students and granted permission for the publication of his biography. It seems unlikely that Gerritsen knew of his colleague's history, but, as it happens, they were never on good terms.

Liberation, 1945

Between 13–16 April battalions of the Canadian 2nd Infantry division attacked Groningen as part of Operation Plunder which was intended to isolate the German army in the west of the Netherlands. The city was held by about 6,000 German combatants, a force which included police units, Dutch and Belgian SS, railway and camp personnel. The Canadians, regular troops, numbered between 6–7,000 but they had to contend against the city defences and, because of its inhabitants, they could not simply destroy everything that got in their way. In the end, only a little more than a hundred civilians were killed and about 270 buildings damaged beyond repair.

Groningen celebrated its liberation enthusiastically. It started modestly, as it was only on 5 May that General Johannes Blaskowitz, commander of the Wehrmacht in the Netherlands, surrendered. However, the celebration turned into a grand event as the month progressed. By the official liberation day, festivities were already taking place in the ruins of the Grote Markt. During the day the citizens played football with the Canadians and at night the orchestra played music in the Nieuwe Kerk. In a liberation event that took place a few days later a procession of 6,000 people wended its way through the city. It was not long before the first criticisms were expressed. On 18 May, the local newspaper stated that it was time to halt excessive revelry: 'cycling through this city, it seems as if every day is a Sunday'. This did not have the impact its writer hoped for as the summer of 1945 was spent in great rejoicing.

Autumn brought with it a different outlook on life. The cheerful mood wore off and people sobered up to face the many difficulties preceding a return to normal existence. This was accompanied by a sense of disillusionment, an awareness that the great plans which had been devised during the occupation had not been realistic. Many felt bitter, not only about injustices that had been done to people during the war, but also about injustices suffered to let go of that past. The reorganisation of a liberated country called for painful decisions which put an end to easy notions of a better, stronger and more stable homeland. About 120 surviving Jews returned to the city. Pieces of their families' furniture were still to be seen in the houses of their neighbours.

After liberation, the university was closed to allow for a 'purification process'. The students blamed the Academic Senate for failing to take a clear moral stance. The senate attempted to defend itself in a letter, but it was too late to repair the negative image it had acquired for being feeble during the war. Furthermore, members of the senate did not present a united front: several reasons led them to have individual perspectives on the future, including the conflicting interests of the various faculties. However, as soon as possible the university tried to pick up where it left off and it prepared for reconstruction and renewal, plans for which had already been made in wartime.

A REFUGE WITH HOMER: STEFAN RADT

Stefan Radt (1927–2017) was born into a Jewish family in Berlin which emigrated to the Netherlands in 1937 to escape persecution. After the German invasion, with the help of Dutch benefactors, Radt went into hiding between 1943 and 1945 during which time he taught himself Greek with the aid of schoolbooks and a text of Homer.

Radt went on to receive his doctorate from the University of Amsterdam in 1958 with a dissertation on Pindar. After a stint in Hamburg working on a classical dictionary, he was appointed to the chair of Ancient Greek at Groningen (1967–87) during which time he edited fragments of the works of Sophocles and Aeschylus. Following his retirement, he was a regular visitor to his friends at the university. One of his most significant publications was completed in this extraordinarily productive period, a ten-volume edition of the *Geography* of Strabo (published between 2002–11) comprising the Greek text and its German translation. International recognition included election as a fellow of the British academy in 1987 and an honorary doctorate from Münster in 2010. He left his extensive library to the university.

COWARDS & HEROES

On 23 June 1945, Groningen was the first Dutch university to reopen its doors. Classes continued for months without a break to make up for lost time. The reopening was not a wholly joyous occasion; many, especially the professors, were ashamed of the university's inactivity during the war. A pamphlet entitled *The Renewal of the University* stated:

It was clear that a noble attitude was expected from the Dutch universities against the occupier's measures. This would not only justify the universities' exalted positions, but would also be seen as an example for the entire population. A large part of the students has shown this by refusing submission, others by choosing deportation above confession. The same cannot be said for the university as a whole and of its teachers. There were those who behaved excellently, but most behaved like civil servants who found themselves in a sticky situation instead of taking on the roles of spiritual leaders or responsible educators.

This was moderately phrased. A newspaper summed up the situation more bluntly as follows:

For the mass of people in the Netherlands there is a clear dichotomy in the academic world: on the one hand there are the professors, who can be described as great cowards. On the other hand, there are the students who are our law-defying heroes. The one side shows the professor, best defined in the terms, 'here I am, thank God, still able to do as I please'; the other side shows the student who answered Germany's first demand with an unrelenting 'no'.

The matter was not that simple, but it became clear that the professors' images were badly damaged. Van der Leeuw, the minister of education and a former rector of Groningen, spoke in a condemnatory manner: 'it is better to have no university, to have empty lecture theatres and plundered laboratories, than to have one that collaborated with the occupier's rules'.

The university's buildings had survived the war largely unscathed and only one, the Anatomical Laboratory, was requisitioned by the Canadian army. On the other hand, staff members had to struggle with a shortage of teaching materials. Some had lost everything, from furniture to washing powder, while others only needed new shoes or a bar of soap. Luckily, humanitarian aid from countries such as France and the UK was able to provide these basic products. Other obstacles included the lack of electricity in some work places and the bad transport connections to the university. People made do with the situation. The Sanskrit professor, Hanna van Lohuizen-de Leeuw, who lived in Leiden, even applied for a seat on a state flight that flew once in two weeks between Schiphol and Eelde (the airport near Groningen), to continue her teaching.

The situation of the students was worse. At this time there was not enough accommodation for all of them. Bicycles were not easily obtainable. The professors were concerned that many students had been removed from the university for so long, or had endured so many hardships in the Netherlands or Germany, that they would be unable to continue studying. Combertus Willem van der Pot, professor of law and the first post-occupation rector, writing in the inaugural edition of the resurrected *Der Clercke Cronike* emphasized the need to start taking studying seriously again, even though the future of the country and the university was unsure. The Netherlands needed fresh graduates.

QUEEN WILHELMINA'S GIFT

A work that spanned the war years was the making of the stained-glass windows in the Aula of the Academy Building. This occupied the artist Johan Dijkstra (1896–1978), a founding member of the De Ploeg (The Plough) association, at different times between 1937 and 1951. The central window (over the door on to the balcony) was a gift from

Queen Wilhelmina who unveiled it in 1938. This led to a commission for Dijkstra to install the other windows.

Dijkstra had a reverential view of education. Regarding the Aula he wrote: 'this is not a church, it is true; yet as we enter it, we set foot within the realm of the spirit; it is a place where we reflect on the true values of our existence'. The gravity may in part be explained by the period in which he was working. As a prompt to reflection, he offered a cycle of windows which dealt with the origins and history of the university. The queen's window depicts two female figures, philosophy and science, laced through with a Greek quotation from Plutarch and surmounted with a five-pointed star representing the unity of the faculties of Theology, Law, Medicine, Philosophy and Arts. Its crowned *W* recalls its donor, who had been given an honorary doctorate in 1914.

The first window on the left tells the story of the Frisian Asegas, twelve guardians of the oral law who refused Charlemagne's command to write their lore down. They were cut adrift at sea in a boat with no rigging. Remembering the prayers of St Willibrord (who had come from Northumbria in England to convert the Frisians) they realised that there was a thirteenth man in the boat: Christ guided them to shore where his staff lit up as a fiery beacon for future sailors. He enjoined them to follow the emperor's command and thus, on the right-hand side, we see a young man writing. Odin's ravens fly about his head as pagan and Christian traditions meet.

Charlemagne

The second window continues this story as Ludger, 'heavenly light of Friesland' converts the Frisians. At the top of the window, the Cistercians labour. The third window has another man of light, Wessel Gansfort (see page 3). This window also depicts Aduard humanists such as Agricola (page 4) along with Praedinius (page 5) and images of medieval Groningen. The university era is heralded in in the fourth window with Petrus Camper (page 45) and J.C. Kapteyn (page 71). The smaller figures are celebrated Groningen scholars including Ubbo Emmius (page 8), Franciscus Gomarus (page 15), Johann Bernoulli (page 41), Sybrandus Stratingh (page 66), Aletta Jacobs, Petrus Hofstede de Groot (page 67) and Gerard Heymans (page 73). The then recently murdered Leonard Polak (page 94) also appears. To these worthies are added 'various student types' embracing the proud, the pious and the materialist. In a rare instance of levity, one scholar announces *multa scripsi* (much have I written) to which his colleague replies, *plura bibsi* (more have I drunk).

POLEMOLOGY: BERT RÖLING

Between 1961 and 1993 Groningen had a Polemology Institute for the study of the causes of war. It was founded by B.V.A. (Bert) Röling (1906–85) who had been

appointed professor of criminal law in 1949, professor of international law in 1957, and professor of peace research in 1972. Röling had been inspired by his role as a judge in the international military tribunal in Japan and his experience as a delegate to the UN.

Röling was born into a Catholic family in 's-Hertogenbosch and thus began his study of law at Nijmegen (a Catholic university) where he was conferred with his MA. Dissatisfied with the religion of his upbringing and with the university, he went on to study at Marburg an der Lahn and at Utrecht where he received his doctorate *cum laude* in 1933. There he was one of the founders of the Criminological Institute and, amongst other things, he wrote – in Dutch – *The Criminological Significance of Shakespeare's Macbeth* (1946). From 1936 he had practical experience as a judge in Dutch courts. This could not fully prepare him for his years as a war-crimes judge in Tokyo (1946–8) where he returned a dissenting opinion that differed from that of his colleagues (and The Hague). These years kindled his interest in international law.

Back in the Netherlands, he was appointed professor at Groningen. He never shunned controversy and went on to be critical of Dutch foreign policy (and this affected his career) and, more popularly, to oppose atomic weapons and American intervention in Vietnam. He became a major figure in the international peace movement. His advocacy of peace was unsurprising given that at Tokyo he had noted that 'it is generally recognised that in every war – war crimes are committed by soldiers of every army. No government or commander will be able to prevent all war crimes'. When Dutch politics shifted he was, in 1973, offered the position of under-secretary of state for peace and security, which he turned down as it would have required him to put aside his teaching and research.

CHAPTER TEN

MUSEUMS

I N 1815 Prof. Theodorus van Swinderen (1784–1851) began a collection that would become the core of the university's natural history museum. It holdings related to geology and zoology along with the cabinet of curiosities of Petrus Camper and his son which had been presented to Groningen by King Willem I in 1820. The Camper collection had medical specimens of all kinds, including the eyeball of an elephant, a turtle's scrotum and a large variety of embryos. The king later gifted the university with the collection of Pieter de Riemer (1769-1831), a physician from The Hague. This included almost a thousand objects, many of which were skulls since de Riemer was interested in the correlation between brain size and intellectual ability (he was a phrenologist).

In 1833, the anatomy collection was housed in the hospital in the Munnekholm where, supplemented by wax and papier-mache models, it was used for teaching. Later in the century it was broken into two divisions, pathology, and general anatomy and embryology. These two collections were moved to the Oostersingel hospital in 1903. Superseded in their instructional functions, the pathology collection and the general collection were absorbed into the University Museum before 2003.

Such was the distinction of the natural history collection that it was moved to the 1850 Academy Building. Prof. Hendrik Jan van Ankum became its curator in 1872 and he did much to augment and display the collection. The 1906 fire in the Academy Building destroyed it (helped, no doubt, by the alcohol used to preserve some of the specimens).

COLLECTION OF COLLECTIONS

It was not until 1934 that the current University Museum opened, the brainchild of the then rector Antoon Gerard Roos, following the examples of the universities of Leiden and Utrecht. Roos requested and received many donations of items from professors and alumni. The portraits, instruments, apparatus and documents Roos collected were deposited in the Corps de Garde (a building that is now a hotel on the corner of Oude Boteringestraat and Lopende Diep). This closed a decade later due to the war and when it reopened in 1949 it was relocated to the Academy Building. From there, it made one further move: in 1987 it transferred to its current site in the Zwanestraat (near the university's library), a facility that was rebuilt in 2004.

The museum has assumed the guardianship of a number of other university collections that have considerably diversified its holdings. This process begun in the 1980s when it took over the Botanical Museum. In 2003, this was followed by the collections of the Ethnological Museum and the

◄ Anatomy specimens

Anatomy Collection

Anatomical Museum. The Natural History Museum was placed under its guardianship in 2007. In addition, the University Museum is responsible for the art in the Academy Building, including the portraits of professors in the Senate Room.

The museum has more than 8,000 ethnological objects in its care. The origin of this collection lies in the benefaction of Theodore Pieter van Baaren (1912–1989), a Groningen professor of theology who founded the *Volkenkundig Museum Gerardus van der Leeuw* (operational between 1978 and 2003), and who had a particular interest in New Guinea. Van Baaren named the museum after one of his predecessors, Van der Leeuw (1890–1950), who had been a pioneer in the history of religion. The Van der Leeuw Museum subsequently acquired custodianship of the Princessehof collection of the city of Leeuwarden (which is focused on the Dutch East Indies), and a colonial agricultural collection given by the city of Deventer.

The University Museum has been working on a digitisation process to make its collection more accessible. It can be visited online at the Dutch Ethnological Collection Foundation's website: <www.svcn.nl>. This technological advance has its precursor in the museum's antique stereoscopes, wooden boxes into which one looks through two observation holes whose lenses create an image with a 3-D effect.

HENDRIK JACOBUS JUT (1851-78)

All that remains of the head of Hendrik Jacobus Jut is a plaster cast since the original, once held in the museum, eventually rotted away. Jut's head was a specimen of a criminal type. In 1872, with the help of Christien Goedvolk whom he subsequently married, Jut murdered a rich widow and her maid during a robbery. The proceeds financed the couple's brief stays in New York and in South Africa. However, they were unhappy abroad and felt safe enough to return to Rotterdam where they opened a coffee house. There, Jut incautiously let slip the source of his capital and he was sentenced to life imprisonment for murder while his wife was imprisoned for theft. He survived in Leeuwarden prison for a little over two years.

CROCODILES IN STORAGE

The greater part of the museum's holdings is stored in its depot. New objects that arrive there must first be kept in a freezer for a few days to kill any bacteria or other creatures on or in them. A selection procedure takes place according to several criteria: one is that the artefacts must be linked to the university in some way; another is that they must be in a reasonable state since if they are too decrepit they are destroyed.

The depot consists of two areas for wet and dry storage. The wet storage is for objects that must be stored in fluids. Numerous moveable racks contain hundreds of glass jars with biological samples such as plants, animals, and human body parts. All these are stored in an alcoholic solution which can keep them intact for many years. Sometimes the solution needs to be refreshed or new plugs are required.

The dry storage contains a broad diversity of objects, including a car, an iron lung, an antique closet and one of the first computers. This area also has several moveable racks that contain stuffed animals, such as crocodiles, chickens, owls, and even a Javanese lapwing (a critically endangered bird). A few moveable stacks in the dry storage are filled with human skulls from different centuries and continents which were used to research the origins of humankind. The geology collection is even more extensive: it contains 60–70,000 stones. New additions are made to the collection every year, especially scientific instruments from the university's laboratories.

VISITING

The museum is open to the public and there is no charge to enter. It arranges educational tours for primary and secondary schools. In addition to its regularly changing current exhibitions, there are permanent exhibitions of anatomy specimens, scientific instruments and objects from the ethnological collection. A room is given over to the history of Dr Aletta Jacobs.

CHAPTER ELEVEN

1950-2000: EXPANSION

THE Netherlands passed a new Higher Education Act in June 1949. Its most important stipulations included extended autonomy for the universities, expansion of the teaching and support staff and the raising of salaries. A national Higher Academic Board was instituted to monitor university collaborations. The new act was the successor of the one of 1876 that had been in force up to this point. It was a miracle that the nineteenth-century legislation had endured so long, despite the drastic changes in Dutch society. In 1876 around 1,000 prosperous students attended the three universities. By 1950 this number had grown to 26,379 (of whom 4,088 were women), from all classes of society. The Dutch population had increased from four to ten million in this period. Society's perception of universities had changed, and this change was recognised in the new act. An intellectual education was no longer the only issue: the moral shaping of students and the promotion of social responsibility was to play an important part in university life.

The first years of economic recovery were over. However, at the start of the 1950s, the Netherlands was still not flourishing. Parliament frequently debated subjects to do with poverty and malnutrition among students. There was even an increase in tuberculosis in the universities. Despite legislation, lack of money kept working-class children from studying.

THREE COMPLEXES

In 1958 the first comprehensive post-war building scheme was designed, the 'three complexes plan'. It was envisioned that the university would concentrate in the city centre (around the Academy Building), the hospital area, and a new location outside of the city. The latter was the then barely developed Paddepoel, which would later become the Zernike Campus and house a science faculty which needed much more room than the city centre could supply. The three complexes plan was, broadly speaking, eventually realised. The biologists, who needed good soil, could not move to Paddepoel because of unsuitable clay in the ground there. Instead, they located to Haren and the Hortus Botanicus. The astronomers were also unhappy with Paddepoel because of the city lights, so they moved to Roden for a while.

By 1964 over 6,200 students were registered in Groningen. The increase brought about a need for new facilities: a special restaurant with cheap meals for students was opened, a canteen was built, and a subsidised recreation centre was founded. In the fifties and early sixties there was extensive discussion about student accommodation and adequate teaching space. Where was the ever-growing number of students to be housed and how would this be paid for? Throughout the 1960s more than half of the students lived in lodgings and were financially dependent on their parents. In 1960 the first student flat was opened by the Foundation for Student Housing. Students were able to rent a room for a relatively low price. The conditions were quite different from

◄ *Entrance to the Harmony Complex*

Queen Juliana receives an honorary doctorate in the Martinikerk (1964)

present-day student flats, as they included janitors who would occasionally peel pota-toes and even clean shoes!

In 1976, with student numbers over 13,000, the university presented a plan that was intended to solve all housing problems for the following ten to fifteen years. The uni-versity would be housed in five areas: the city centre (the Harmony Building, the Acad-emy Building and Boteringestraat), the Hortus, the Bodenterrein (Antonius Deusing-laan), Paddepoel, and Haren. This plan would provide the university with an additional 75,000m² of space. The costs were estimated at 225 million guilders. The fact that some houses would have to be demolished was not well received by residents in the Hortus area, residents who today, still worry about smaller university expansions.

BABY BOOMERS

By the 350th anniversary of the university in 1964 radical changes were under way. The Dutch population was almost 11.5 million and around this time the baby boom genera-tion had reached the university. Pipe-smoking gentlemen were replaced by jeans-wear-ing, tobacco-rolling and paper-reading activists. Along with the pipe-smoking gentle-men, the everlasting student was endangered. This had typically been a young man from a wealthy background who could move out of his parents' house to study for a decade. After these ten years' labour, he would graduate and automatically be offered a great job. Although this type had become rare after the war, the average student still spent seven or eight years at university. This lengthy period of study had become a problem. The government kept proposing ways to shorten it, but students as well as professors were not enamoured of these ideas.

Many had believed that simply registering for a degree did not make one a student. Only having become a member of a student society could one could call oneself a stu-dent. Being a student was not just about studying; it involved a certain manner of living, a degree of 'civilisation' that only a student association could provide. In such circles, it had been thought, young people could receive the kind of education that would prepare them for a social position. Studying began with applying to a society, going through its hazing process, becoming acquainted with the city and only then visiting the registrar to be enrolled for a subject. Such people were more connected to their society than to the university. In Groningen the most prominent societies were the fraternity Vindicat and the sorority Magna Pete. However, a growing number of new arrivals, called 'nihilists', opted not to be members of any society.

The desire for reformation in the student world was a national phenomenon. In Amsterdam for example, all societies were gathered under one umbrella. At Nijmegen it became compulsory for all students to become a member of one of their existing associations. In Groningen change manifested itself most clearly in the sports association, *De Groene Uil*. Magna Pete was also eager for transformation and discussed combining with others, such as VERA (*Veri et recti amici,* true and honest friends). Yet there was resistance against amalgamating societies as well. Just as before the war, the Catholic student society Albertus Magnus (founded in 1896) was unwilling to have closer ties to Vindicat. Many students from VERA were also opposed to the idea of any fraternisation with Vindicat. Representatives of Vindicat, Magna Pete, Albertus Magnus, VERA, and others came together and discussed the many possibilities. In the end, organising the student body into one community proved too ambitious.

Student protest outside Academy Building (1971)

PROTESTS

In 1968 Parisian student protests culminated in *les évènments*, with its riots and police tear gas. The student movement had many international followers, including in the Netherlands where there was the extra priming of the Amsterdam riots of 1966 (which had not been specifically linked to students, but which commanded worldwide attention when a harmless but very visible smoke bomb went off during the wedding celebrations of Princess Beatrix to Claus von Amsberg, a German consort who was then, *ipso facto*, a controversial choice of husband).

When student protests broke out all over Europe and the US in 1968 the Dutch had their share of demonstrations, the most famous of which was the 1969 sit-in of the offices of the University of Amsterdam (occupied again as recently as 2015). Student protests in the Netherlands were generally a little milder than in other countries, but they were nonetheless successful since change in Dutch universities was more substantial. Pressured by these incidents, the minister of the Catholic Community Party (KVP) presented a memorandum to the House of Representatives, describing a new system of academic governance. This memorandum would be the basis for the Law of Academic Board Reformation (WUB) that was passed in 1970. The WUB introduced more participation in university governance for students and staff.

Comparatively few occupations or other spectacular actions took place in Groningen, but debates were a daily activity. The Academy Building was occupied in 1968 and several times thereafter (so much so that the gestures lost their impact). Changes in university management progressed steadily, although the rate at which it did so differed from faculty to faculty. The University Board now negotiated with the students, which gave it the image of being progressive.

In the 1970s, when the student population topped 16,000, a whole range of organisations and groups grew up that frequently did not want anything to do with one another. Consequently, students picked one group that interested them and that became the basis of their social life. Leftist students, for example, often participated

The Harmony Building. In the square stands Marte Röling's detumescent Non scholae sed vitae *(1999), whose title reminds passers-by that study is for the sake of life and not examinations*

in the squatter movement, the anti-nuclear energy movement, or groups supporting developing countries. To be part of such a body involved the creation of a sense of identity. Overall, student movements fragmented and individualised.

This eventful time of involved student movements ended around 1980. The squatter riots at the coronation of Queen Beatrix in Amsterdam in 1980 sounded their death-knell. Although squatters and radicals still existed, they lost their grip on the mass of students who no longer identified with the violence that had become associated with them. Leftist ideals did not disappear entirely from student culture, but they made room for more career-oriented attitudes. Furthermore, students were turning towards the international world. The rise of organisations such as AEGEE (*Association des Etats Généraux des Etudiants de l'Europe*), the European Students' Forum, founded in 1985, was an example of this (Groningen houses one of its many branches).

AMONG & ABOVE PROFESSORS

Willem Frederik Hermans (1921–95) was an author and academic from Amsterdam. He studied spatial sciences at the university there and graduated *cum laude* in 1955. He worked as a lecturer in geography at Groningen between 1958 and 1973. In 1975 Hermans published one of his most important novels, *Onder Professoren* (Among Professors). This satirical *roman à clef* dealt with his years of frustration working at Groningen and he portrayed the institution as a collection of timid academic layabouts. He also attacked the university in newspaper interviews. In a 1973 article he caricatured the new democratised system:

> Since democratisation it has become obligatory for people to waste their time tittle-tattling and jabbering. Imagine you need a rubber band. This will cost you about a day of debating ... You need to send application letters to get something done. These are sent to institutions that have nothing to do with the situation and so a second letter is required. Professors are not business people, so they are incapable of dictating a letter to a secretary. I know professors who spend hours writing drafts with pencils. This costs a fortune.

Hermans's novel may have inspired the title *Boven Professoren* (Above Professors, 1995) by Marjolein Mandersloot given to an art installation in the offices of the Board of the University. These twenty-four bronze Venetian-style masks were purchased in 1995 and they reminded supplicant professors of the university hierarchy. An official guide to the art of the university states that it is 'doubtful' that the masks symbolise deceit or night (which conceals vice).

DISHARMONY

Nothing in the late twentieth-century history of the university drew so much national attention as the demolition of the *Harmonie* Building, which currently houses the faculties of Arts and Law. The Harmony had been a community centre and concert hall in the city centre. It had extraordinary acoustic qualities and was of great historic and architectural value. The university first expressed its interest in it as early as 1948 when plans were drawn up to house the Faculty of Arts there. After some time, it became clear that the university was not willing to pay the asking price for the property and things were put on hold. It was only in 1963 that the university acquired the Harmony site after the city council had first purchased it. In the short period it took to complete these transactions the first protests were made. Prominent figures both from the architectural and musical fields were against the demolition of the concert hall and signed a petition for its preservation. They were not only supported by citizens of Groningen, but also by national newspapers. However, except for the Farmers' Party, the city council continued to support the sale.

The discussion became really heated when the Harmony was placed on the national list of historic buildings in 1967. This stated that 'the concert hall is one of the best-preserved examples of nineteenth-century architecture that our country has to offer'. After this, the mayor of Groningen, J.J.A. Berger, was compelled to travel to The Hague to explain personally to the minister of culture why he was so intent on destroying it. The minister, M.A.M. Klompé, subsequently removed the building from the list of historic buildings and issued a demolition permit.

Just when the university had finally had its way, it became clear that the building was actually too small to house the entire Faculty of Arts so plans were changed, leading many to question the purpose of removing it. In 1969 a final attempt was made to preserve the concert hall. The idea was floated that it could become a cultural centre that would form a bridge between the city and the university. This plan, however, was rejected. In 1972 the university demolished the old building almost entirely and now only its front remains. It was not clear what was going to be done with the newly cleared site. Four years later the university, in cooperation with the city council, drew up plans to create a University House with multiple functions. It would provide offices for the Law Faculty and the Department of Psychology as well as a large restaurant, student unions, and centres for cultural education and spiritual well-being. This plan for a dynamic University House was never realised.

In 1978 the new government announced cutbacks that also affected the plans for the complex. Building costs had to be curtailed severely, which meant that the student unions, the library and cultural institutions would not be receiving new and expensive accommodation. When it was established that the University Library would be constructed on the Broerstraat instead of in the Hortus area, this had significant consequences for the Harmony site. Because the new library would be nearby, the ministry insisted that the Faculty of Arts should be housed there. Faced with even more cutbacks, the university decided to fall in with the wishes of the government and it installed the faculties of Arts and Law. In doing this, the university returned to its original plans of 1948.

A major – but uncontroversial – change at the Harmony is scheduled for 2020 when the Faculty of Law will move to what is currently the city's public library on the Oude Boteringestraat. After this, the Harmony will undergo extensive renovations which will involve incorporating Arts Faculty offices that are spread around different sites in the city centre.

Eighties

The oil crisis of 1979 marked the end of twenty years of immense economic growth, but not the growth of the university which had 18,000 students by 1990. In the last two decades of the twentieth century the university underwent significant changes: almost every study programme was subject to new regulations.

One of the biggest changes in the 1980s was The Hague's policy concerning students who took too long to complete their studies. These cost the universities a lot of money. For example, in the Department of Physics students often took more than eight years to complete a degree. This had to become more efficient, so many study programmes were thoroughly evaluated and reorganised. In several cases, the formal duration of study was reduced to five years. In practice, however, students still took longer. The reasons for this included failing exams, internships that did not fit into the academic timetable, or extracurricular activities that took up too much time. Furthermore, studying abroad for a couple of months or even a year became very popular. While lecturers had no problem with this length of study, the administrators did.

Students of English (1978)

The two-phase structure was introduced in 1982. All programmes were shortened to four years and student grants were tied to this duration. This meant that students that took too long to finish would have their grants stopped. In most cases, the shortened programmes were designed by making students begin their specialisation earlier, which limited the range of programmes. The *kandidaatsexamen* was abolished, and instead the propaedeutic phase, or orientation phase, was instated. Many students and staff considered the four-year duration of study to be too short. According to the professor of physics, Jan Carel Francken (1919–2007), it was impossible for him to teach his students properly in a mere four years, which he believed led to a failure to meet reasonable standards of teaching.

Part of the two-phase structure was that a limited number of students were able to move on to the second phase after graduating from the first. In 1982, however, it was still not entirely clear what the second phase should be. The selection of students for this phase also needed to be clarified. Student selection had been a controversial issue ever since the 1960s. Because making education accessible to everyone was important to many political parties, they were unsure as to how exactly selection could be introduced. Eventually, selection through an application procedure was agreed upon. The second phase was shaped by allowing a student to obtain a four-year position as an AIO (*assistent in opleiding* or assistant in training). These assistants were paid by the universities or by private institutions, and their training concluded with the conferral of a PhD. The university continues to have such salaried doctoral candidates, but students without these positions can still register for a PhD. The salaried positions are governed by the *Collective Labour Agreement* of Dutch Universities (*CAO NU*).

To ensure all these changes were adhered to, visitation committees were established. These consisted of professors and students from within the field of study but from other universities who monitored the quality of education, research and organisation. Moreover, they compared the programmes from all Dutch universities and looked at similar programmes around the world. Based on their results, they made specific recommendations for improvements and universities generally followed their suggestions.

CHANGING PROGRAMMES

From 1960 onwards, the government stimulated universities to expand their topics of study and to offer different trajectories within study programmes. In the 1970s, the university also started offering part-time courses. Consequently, there was an enormous expansion of subjects in the 1980s and 1990s. In 1982 the university began courses in computer science, cultural anthropology, business, and modern Greek. A year later it added medieval studies and Roman studies. However, the curriculum threatened to get too diverse. In 1983 the government issued an instruction that the range of programmes in the Netherlands had to be cut back. This meant that an 'exotic' area of study could only be offered at one university. For Groningen this entailed the abolition of cultural anthropology almost as quickly as it had started. In 1983, for instance, the geology department was closed and from then on, the subject was taught in Utrecht and Amsterdam. Things worked the other way around as well: pharmacy was closed in Amsterdam and Leiden in 1985, while it continued to exist in Groningen and Utrecht.

However, some new areas flourished in the 1980s, notably the Faculty of Business, founded in 1986, which immediately became very popular. This was also true for the Faculty of Economics, which had more than 3,300 students by 1990. The enormous growth of the number of students in economics and business was due to several factors. Firstly, the economy was finally recovering from the crisis of the 1970s and early 1980s. Secondly, the notions of management and business lost the negative connotations they had acquired in the 1960s and 1970s.

ASSASSINATION: PIM FORTUYN

One of the most famous (or infamous) modern staff members at Groningen was Wilhelmus Simon Petrus Fortuijn, better known as Pim Fortuyn (1948–2002). He studied sociology at both of Amsterdam's universities where he immersed himself in Marxist theory and was engaged in student politics. He also had the opportunity to participate in the city's gay life. In 1972 he became a research assistant at Groningen and in 1980 he was awarded his PhD, not without some turbulence, but without any question of his academic ability. Fortuyn was employed in the Department of Sociology at the university for another eight years and then resigned to work in public administration.

After this he had a varied career which included stints as a columnist, a professor at Rotterdam, a guru and a political commentator. He combined a deliberately flamboyant public persona and criticism of the political establishment. In 2001 he became the leader of the populist *Leefbaar* (liveable) *Nederland* party which he had to leave the following year because of his strident criticism of Islam, his call to review asylum policy (as the Netherlands was 'full up') and his questioning of the Dutch constitution's prohibition against religious discrimination. His solution to his changed circumstances was to found his own party which he called after himself.

On 6 May, a week before the national elections that might well have made him a key player in parliament, he was shot dead in Hilversum by a 'lone wolf' animal-rights advocate, Volkert van der Graaf (who was sentenced to eighteen years' imprisonment for an – in the Netherlands – unheard of political murder). Had he lived, Fortuyn would have been amongst the most intelligent and colourful of international populist politicians and tested his public's support for a visibly rich intellectual and his King Charles spaniels. In the longer term, his interest in historical and social forces might have led him to consider the famous words attributed to Pastor Niemöller, and to reflect whether, as a highly visible member of a minority himself, there was a black and white answer to Dutch social problems and whether hatred and fear are emotions that spend themselves on particular targets, before, with their work done, they dissolve away leaving harmony and good tailoring behind them.

Porters, Harmony Building

STUDENT ECONOMICS

Despite fierce student protests the 1980s also brought about an increase in tuition fees. In 1982 they were raised to 900 guilders (€408), in 1983 to 1,050 guilders (about €476), in 1985 to 1,350 guilders (€612), and in 1988 to 1,750 guilders (€794). Because of the continuous rise in fees, a new student grant law was passed in 1986. This made university accessible to everyone who had completed HBS or *gymnasium* (pre-university education), regardless of parental income. Everyone from royal princes to working-class children had a right to the same education. Additionally, students were able to take out a loan that was dependent on their parents' earnings.

Students devised a way to pay their tuition fees: part-time employment. Nowadays, many students have a part-time job, but in the 1980s and 1990s this was still relatively new. Slowly but surely, students began to view their studies less as a full-time activity and they set aside more time to earn a little money. This trend has continued to this day when only a minority of students is engaged with full-time study. Most would rather work than take out a loan and there is the added advantage that valuable non-academic lessons are to be learnt outside study programmes. There are fewer options open to students who do not speak Dutch as much of the casual employment in the service industry is closed off for them.

The length of time given to study has thus undergone two cutbacks, an official one shortening the length of degrees, and an unofficial one related to students' paid work.

Some programmes are now impractical: there is not time to acquire new languages, repeat laboratory methods or tackle longer texts.

MACROECONOMICS: ANGUS MADDISON

A British economist, Maddison (1926–2010) studied at Cambridge, McGill University and Johns Hopkins. His international education prepared him for an even more international experience of employment. While an analyst for the OECD he was involved with projects dealing with Brazil, Guinea, Mongolia, the USSR and Japan. Between leaving the OECD and taking up a professorship in economics at Groningen (1978–97), his work took him to Pakistan and Ghana. Maddison was very positive about his work environment in the university which gave him the freedom to follow his own research plans and where he mainly taught graduate students. He was a co-founder of the GGDC, the Groningen Growth and Development Centre, which reflected his background in questions of long-term economic development (one of his books was titled *Chinese Economic Performance in the Long Run, 1-2030* where *1* was AD1 and *2030* a date safely in the future). Maddison stressed the historical significance of Asian economies, so he was unsurprised at the growth of these in his own time. His work is continued by the GGDC where the Maddison Project Database was updated in 2018 and includes long-term data on income levels for 169 countries.

THE COMMERCIAL UNIVERSITY

The magic word of the 1990s was 'modularisation'. This involved all study programmes being converted into short modules or 'blocks'. Study delays were to be prevented by fitting education into bite-size chunks. The new system also made it easier for students to follow courses in other faculties. This was an international trend. One important advantage was that a student was not faced with a mass of final exams during which a headache might obliterate a year's work or more. On the other hand, there is clear evidence that many students forget the material from a module once it is over. The obvious solution of a hybrid system has not yet been tried. In 1991 a trimester system was implemented and the academic year was divided into three equal periods of classes and exams. This division was eventually replaced by the current system of semesters. What remained constant is that the academic year was typically longer than those of anglophone countries.

When the Dutch economy had recovered in the 1990s, the university again expanded its programs of study. In 1991 journalism and technical business studies were established and these were joined by cognitive science in 1992. The growth of programmes had increasingly less to do with an interest in theoretical study; instead, universities started to fit their course offering to the demands of employers. Ever since the recession of the 1980s, work prospects played a big part in a student's choice of a particular subject.

One professor, the physicist Jan Kommandeur (1929-2012), remarked on the different faces of the university that he had witnessed. First there had been a socially elite university, then a conciliar one, and lastly there was a commercial university. This was partly due to the increasing involvement of industry in financing research, but also because of the way the university began to function like a company. Students came to be viewed as products that were to be turned out as quickly as possible once they were ready and filled up with the requisite knowledge, or the appearance of it.

The 1990s heralded another change in student culture. After the socially-involved students of the 1970s and the career-oriented 1980s, the last decade of the twentieth century saw the rise of a new type of student. The career-oriented mindset of the 1980s still existed, but students were absorbed in a more hedonistic climate where they could have fun. The students of Groningen in the 1990s wanted it all: study grants without loans, a part-time job without study delays, and social lives that at times could make them forget what they were doing in Groningen.

NESTOR

The university purchased its first computer in 1958, a colossal and cumbersome machine. One of the most important developments of the 1980s and 1990s was the general spread of personal computers and the Internet. In December 2000, a university-wide digital learning environment, the first in the country, received the go-ahead. This did not take place without some fears on the parts of students and professors alike. An early concern was that digital learning environments such as Blackboard would eventually replace teaching staff altogether. Another worry was that in navigating the website, students would have to click a mouse so often that they would develop repetitive strain injury. While these concerns were not really taken seriously, there were still some actual problems (including repetitive strain injury), to deal with.

For Blackboard to become an important facility for all faculties required that all members of the university had easy access to the Internet. However, in 2000 there were only 1,500 computers available in the entire campus. In the following years more PCs were acquired, the Internet became increasingly accessible, and since autumn 2008 students and staff members have access to their own virtual workplace wherever they are in the world. Blackboard has been customised for Groningen and is called Nestor, after a wise king in Homer (a trace of the past, but not an unambiguous one since in *The Odyssey* Nestor cannot provide the critical information he is asked for). The punch card driven machine of 1958 has given way to high-performance computing running on a 4368-core cluster with 436TB of disk space. Virtual reality facilities are used for everything from astronomy to treating phobias. The Centre for Information Technology is based in the Zernike Complex in a building which, in 2014, was renamed the Smitsborg after Donald W. Smit (1919–98) its first director.

Smitsborg (2002)

CHAPTER TWELVE

2000-2018: MILLENNIUM

THE new millennium was marked with the implementation of the Bologna Declaration which entailed changing the structure of all bachelor and master-level degree programmes. This facilitated internationalisation, an important element in current university planning. Although the university is financially sound, it is a large and diverse institution with many competing demands on its resources (in 2017 it had a budget of €800 million). The amount of money to be allocated to new faculties, buildings, permanent staff and international links have all involved debate, progress and setbacks. In the background is the shifting political landscape of Dutch education policy. It does not shift violently, but there are significant changes; for example, it was decided that first year student fees for bachelor's degrees were halved in 2018–19.

BOLOGNA: BACHELOR & MASTER, 2002

One of the first major steps towards an increasingly internationally oriented university was the introduction of bachelor's and master's degrees following the Bologna Declaration (which the Netherlands signed in 1999). The goal of this agreement was to synchronise study programmes in European countries and thus facilitate student exchange. The degree structure it introduced was fundamentally different from the traditional Dutch *doctoraal* degree in that it consists of two phases: an undergraduate and a graduate one, ending with a bachelor's and a master's degree respectively (the *doctoraal*, in contrast, consisted of a four-year programme after which students received the title *doctorandus*). Naturally, the switch from the old system was accompanied by many uncertainties. At first, existing *doctoraal* programmes were simply adapted to the new model, and in 2002 the university awarded the first bachelor's degree, while the traditional *doctoraal* remained in place until the end of August 2007. Today, all programmes are organized to meet the Bologna norms.

Additionally, the university uses the European Credit Transfer and Accumulation System (ECTS) to indicate the workload of a given course and thus make programmes internationally comparable. However, there are still many aspects of degrees that are peculiar to individual countries. The Dutch grading system, in which the maximum grade of 10 is rarely awarded, can lead to misinterpretations abroad, because a result of eight or nine may not look like a great accomplishment for those who grade with percentages while the numbers are too high for American-style SAT tests. The combination of the ECTS workload of modules and the notes explaining the Dutch grading system which are now found on degree certificates is a step towards internationally communicable standards.

RESEARCH

The university seeks to be a top institution for research and it has approximately 2,000 PhD students. It recently adopted three social themes as research focuses: energy, healthy ageing and sustainable society. Energy is the domain of engineering and

◄ Nijenborg 6, Zernike Campus

science; healthy ageing involved the medical, natural and social sciences along with economics; and sustainable society describes itself in an official publication as 'a network organisation for all Social Sciences and Humanities research'. It is impossible in a diverse institution the size of Groningen to reduce all research to three categories no matter how broadly they can interpreted, so there are institutes based in all of the faculties in addition to inter-faculty institutes.

In the university's information on 'Leading research' the 'Top publications' section comprises a list of Groningen-authored articles in *Nature* and *Science* and nothing more. While the standing and range of these journals provide a convenient list, this is also emblematic of the relative prestige of the sciences. The 'Top Researchers' section is more varied and lists academics who have been awarded prizes and grants or who have been elected to learned societies (for example, Prof. Lodi Nauta, who works on early-modern philosophy, was awarded a Spinoza Prize in 2016. This is the highest Dutch academic accolade and is worth €2,500,000 with which a laureate can fund a research team).

PERSPIRATION: BEN FERINGA

Bernard Lucas Feringa (b. 1951), who was appointed professor of organic chemistry in 1988, was joint winner of the 2016 Nobel Prize in recognition of his work in nanotechnology. Feringa had completed both his undergraduate and postgraduate study at Groningen during a geographically stable career. He has received invitations to work at other universities, but decided to decline them for family reasons (he is married and has three scientist daughters) and because 'life wasn't bad at Groningen':

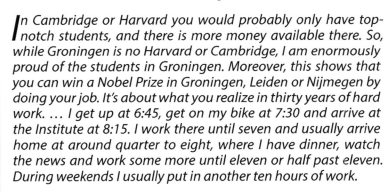

In Cambridge or Harvard you would probably only have top-notch students, and there is more money available there. So, while Groningen is no Harvard or Cambridge, I am enormously proud of the students in Groningen. Moreover, this shows that you can win a Nobel Prize in Groningen, Leiden or Nijmegen by doing your job. It's about what you realize in thirty years of hard work. … I get up at 6:45, get on my bike at 7:30 and arrive at the Institute at 8:15. I work there until seven and usually arrive home at around quarter to eight, where I have dinner, watch the news and work some more until eleven or half past eleven. During weekends I usually put in another ten hours of work.

In 1999 Feringa invented a light propelled molecular motor and his four-wheel drive molecular car appeared on the cover of *Nature* in 2011. Subsequently he worked on nanoscale light switches, artificial muscles and self-repairing materials. He laments that the Netherlands 'invests far too little in fundamental research and chemistry' and that as a result it could fall behind competition from countries such as China. The Nobel Prize is only one of the honours he has received: he has been the recipient of the Spinoza Prize, the Royal Society of Chemistry Prize and the inaugural European Chemistry Gold Medal. He is a board member of the Royal Dutch Academy (KNAW) and has been decorated by the king. In 2023 the university's Feringa Building, a new 62,000m^2 university science facility is scheduled to open. Although he has been honoured with a bronze bust, he looks perfectly normal.

Co-Operation

In 2005 the university, the UMCG, the *Hanzehogeschool*, the city and the province of Groningen came together to establish a 'knowledge city' in the north of the Netherlands. Such collaboration is practically demonstrated by the university's science campus which is located at Zernike, a site which is shared with the *Hanzehogeschool* under the name Campus Groningen. The campus aims to be a meeting place of academic talent and the business and technology sectors. Although the institutions' teaching and administrative buildings are clearly badged as separate from one another, there are areas of close co-operation, notably Energy Academy Europe which is housed at Nijenborg 6, a fully sustainable building roofed with solar panels which was opened in 2016. This is the base of the Centre for Isotope Research, the Centre for Energy and Environmental Science, Combustion Technology, Ocean Ecosystems and Geo-energy.

Another area of co-operation is in sport. The ACLO, a student foundation, was established in 1945 and in 2001 it joined with the students of the *Hanzehogeschool*. It incorporates 49 clubs serving almost 20,000 members. Many of the sports are ones to be expected, such as beach volleyball, intertidal hiking and pole-dancing, but there are also unusual activities such as power yoga, salsa, underwater hockey, and Zumba. An equivalent staff organization was established in 1950 and is called SPR Sport.

Energy Academy Europe

China & Yantai 2007–18

In 2007 Prof. Jan van der Harst from the Department of International Relations was appointed academic director of the newly established Dutch Studies Centre that was opened in co-operation with the University of Fudan in Shanghai. Since then, Fudan has offered courses involving the study of the Netherlands. In 2011, a Confucius Institute opened in Groningen. It is part of a global network supported by Hanban (an agency of the Chinese ministry of education) which arranges courses in Chinese language and culture and supports school teaching. The institute is an example of the soft power instanced by the British Council, the Alliance Française or the Anglo-American Institute that opened in Groningen in 1937 (see page 92). Although the Groningen branch of the Institute was originally conceived at the Hanzehogeschool, it has links to the university whose former president, Sibrand Poppema, was elected to the Council of Confucius Institute Headquarters. The year 2011 also saw the establishing of the Tsinghua-Groningen research centre for China-EU relations. In 2016, Prof. Oliver Moore was appointed to a new chair of Chinese language and culture with a view to developing a BA programme in the area. He joined the Arts Faculty's Centre for East Asian Studies which offers an MA on the culture, politics and economics of East Asia.

These developments went comparatively unremarked. By contrast, there was considerable controversy about the university's plans to establish a branch campus in cooperation with the China Agricultural University in the city of Yantai. These proceeded at lightening pace in 2015 under the guidance of Sibrand Poppema. It was envisioned that Groningen would become 'a global university' by establishing the first Dutch campus in China. It was planned to offer Groningen degrees, initially in a range of science subjects. In March 2015 a declaration of intent was signed at an event that was attended by the Dutch prime minister. In October a further agreement was signed at a meeting attended by the king and President Xi Jinping of China. That there might be a Dutch university campus abroad had not been foreseen by any legislators, so an act of parliament was required to allow things to proceed further.

Sceptics and opponents of the plan had a variety of worries. To these it was answered, variously, that the scheme would require no public money from the university or the Dutch taxpayer, that academic quality would be controlled from Groningen, that there would be a Dutch vice-chancellor, and that academic freedom (and its associated practicalities such as Internet access) was a 'non-negotiable condition'. The Chinese stipulation that there would, of course, be a communist party secretary at Yantai took many, but by no means all, by surprise. One of the people disconcerted was the minister for education, Ingrid van Engelshoven.

In December 2017, Prof. Moore was interviewed for *UK*. He was a supporter of the proposal, but he was not part of the management co-ordinating it. He was able to articulate some things more succinctly or bluntly than those framing matters for consumption by the whole university and, indeed, by the country. Asked what he would do were he in China and forbidden to teach a taboo topic he replied:

There are two things I could do. Either I stick to my guns and allow myself to be fired as a martyr for aca-

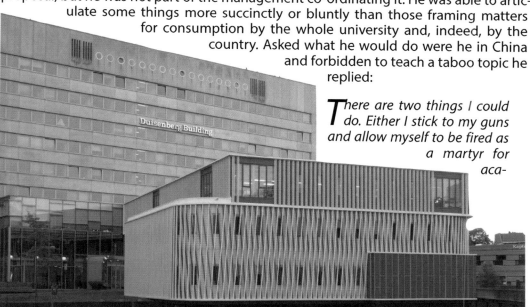

Duisenberg Building (Faculty of Economics & Business)

demic freedom. I don't think that would help much. Or I remain on good terms with this civil servant by leaving the forbidden subjects out of my lectures. But in my own house I'd still be able to say what I want, to whomever I want.

Originally, the University Council (a staff and student body) was merely to be consulted about the Yantai decision but after national discussion and political pressure, it received a power of veto. Some members of the council paid a site visit to Yantai and the plan was re-presented in late 2017, framed in a manner to respond to concerns about it. In January 2018, the majority of votes from the University Council that would be required to endorse the scheme was not forthcoming. After approximately €2,000,000 had been spent on them, the Yantai plans were shelved, although to what extent is not clear to everyone. Senior members of the university (including the rector) have observed that 'for now, we can only observe that the time is perhaps not yet right' while Fu Zetian, vice-chairman of the China Agricultural University Council, subsequently remarked that 'the journey ahead to the successful establishment of UGY [University of Groningen at Yantai] is still long and tough' and speaks of the project in the future tense.

Binding Study Advice, 2009

A significant shift in attitudes to study was initiated in the last decade. The university made clear that what it perceived as some students' laid-back approach to their study had to alter. As Rector Frans Zwarts stated: 'Dutch students have had it incomparably easier than students in Belgium or the United States. Here in Groningen our policy has been that students start to study when they're ready. That needs to change'. Students were thought to be over-invested in demanding social lives that sometimes took priority over their degree programmes. For Dutch students, this was related to the *zesjesmentaliteit* (literally, 'six-mentality'), being satisfied with a pass mark rather than a higher grade (six out of ten was the lowest pass mark).

To counter this, in 2009 the university introduced Binding Study 'Advice' or BSA (the translation is either incompetent or mendacious as it is not advice but a compulsory instruction). This required first year students to pass at least 40 out of 60 EC (study credits in the Bologna system), otherwise, they would be excluded from their programme for two years unless there were special circumstances such as illness etc. In 2013 the requirement was raised to 45 EC and an additional rule was introduced requiring first-years to acquire all points of the first year within two years. Although a cause of considerable anxiety at the time, the BSA has improved pass rates and students who were not suited to a study have been spared two or three years wasted time in a programme they could not finish. On the other hand, some of the university's luminaries had performed poorly at some stages of their studies – striking the right balance in the BSA is revised in an ongoing process.

International and Intercultural

Of the university's 31,000 students, 7,000 are international (2018–19). A third of its academic staff are from abroad. Students and staff represent 120 countries. International students are regarded as assets who bring different perspectives with them, giving added value to Dutch education. They also compensate for a decreasing number of Dutch students, a demographic trend that is expected to have a visible impact in higher education in the Netherlands from 2020 onwards.

The international office, as well as several societies, support foreign students, help them integrate and make their stay in the Netherlands as profitable and enjoyable as possible. For example, the Erasmus Student Network (ESN) runs a mentor programme for foreign students. During the year it arranges 150 activities. Nevertheless, apart from finding housing, which is a universal problem, some visitors mix badly with their Dutch peers. At times, this may be because students from countries that are strongly represented in the university's population, such as Germany and China, can easily form exclusive groups of their own. However, the openness of Dutch students to friendships with international ones has also been questioned. There is very rarely any friction between students on the grounds of nationality, but sometimes Dutch students do not wish to take the trouble of, for example, having a non-Dutch speaker in a flat-share.

The rector, Elmer Sterken, has commented on this: 'I don't believe in forced integration. Of course, you should have some regulations about integration, but there are two sides to internationalisation. I hear a lot about solutions like more mixed classes. But I don't think it's that important. You really cannot enforce integration. It has to happen in its own way'. Still, he stresses the importance of international student societies: 'Even if you can't enforce it, you can open the door for those who do want to participate. By supporting international student organisations, you make it easier for those students who do choose to participate'.

There are also issues from the Dutch side. For example, increasing student numbers put pressure on the accommodation available. The current minister of education, Ingrid van Engelshoven, has remarked on concerns about the accessibility of universities or the choice of programmes for Dutch students in a system where resources are finite. She has established 'the quality of the international classroom' as one of the streams that will get funding from the Comenius Programme (which awards money for the improvement of teaching in higher education).

The university has a branch office in Papenburg, UGNWG (University of Groningen North West Germany). It also has many and changing Erasmus and exchange links with foreign institutions. It In addition, it has several designated partners:

AMERICAS: The National Autonomous University of Mexico, UCLA, the University of Pennsylvania, the University of São Paulo.

ASIA: Bandung Institute of Technology, China Agricultural University, Fudan University, Gadjah Mada University, Osaka University, Peking University, Tsinghua University, the University of Indonesia.

EUROPE: Ghent University, the University of Göttingen, Uppsala University.

Groningen is one of nineteen members of The Guild of European Research-Intensive Universities and a member of the Coimbra Group for established multidisciplinary universities.

DIVERSITY

While discussing internationalization, Minister van Engelshoven characterised Dutch society as outward-looking and diverse and noted that an international classroom brought added value in terms of socialization and personal development as well as different intellectual outlooks and the resultant possibility of broader employment. Remarking on the benefits to personal development prompts the observation that much of what is entailed in successful internationalization can be regarded as a sub-set of an investment in diversity.

Individuals and groups of international members of the university have been the butt of stereotyped jokes which, though for the most part not intended to be offensive, were at least unfortunate. That this happens is hardly surprising: it is typical of all European societies (international staff or students also have negative observations about other internationals as well as about the Dutch). This humour also manifests itself between the inhabitants of different regions of the Netherlands in which there are standard remarks about people from the south, or the west, from Friesland or from Groningen (where the inhabitants have deprecation that they aim at themselves). There are differences then that are not confined to culture. The under-representation of women at professorial grade has been mentioned in Chapter 8, a particularly interesting case since it does not involve a minority group. To this could be added a reasonably long list. For example, the Dutch higher education system is not geared towards older students. At the time of writing, there is work to be done with respect to race, gender, sexuality, religious beliefs and disabilities. Were a fuller list to be thought out it might be easy

The Changing Same by M. Blok & B. Lugthart (2000)

to despair that anything could be done to address all of these vital topics while making the necessary time for education. It might also be objected that since the Netherlands is an egalitarian society, such issues are not pressing. Looking at things another way, under the umbrella of negotiating difference (rather than a specific example of it such as internalization) there is a basic set of dispositions, critical abilities and skills that students could carry on to very different environments in the future and this imperative fits with Dutch universities' promotion of responsible citizenship and the country's extensive anti-discrimination legislation.

Whereas the integration of all sorts of different groups into a department, a faculty or the university is something that would receive broad support at a general level, questions raised by diversity are not straightforward. When does a comment in a class become a disciplinary matter? How tolerant should one be of another person's perceived intolerance or clumsiness? When are others' claims, beliefs or identities to be challenged? Are there particular diversity questions related to specific subject areas or future employment? Investigating some of these issues develops many of the challenges raised by internationalization without shunting them aside and would be in perfect accordance with the university's identification of diversity as a core value in its current strategic plan. Given the expertise available on site, the university can produce its own solutions and devise its own improvements.

ENGLISH AS A LINGUA FRANCA

In view of the rising number of foreign students and staff there has been recurring discussion about making English the official or *de facto* language of the university. In 2000 Prof. Pervez Ghauri of the Faculty of Economics and Business predicted that all students would be studying in English within ten years because this would be more attractive for internationals and open up career prospects for Dutch students. He turned out to be right about his own faculty which switched over to English in 2009. That same year, the rector, Frans Zwarts, delivered his address for the opening of the academic year in English. The university's *Language and Culture Policy* (2015) lists a number of advantages to delivering programmes in English, including increasing the diversity of the students

Qumran & The Dead Sea Scrolls

In 1947 a shepherd accidentally discovered the first of eleven caves at Qumran on the north-west shore of the Dead Sea. The caves preserved manuscripts written on papyrus, leather and copper that dated from the third century BCE to the second century CE. These included the earliest manuscripts of the Hebrew Scriptures along with previously unknown documents of Jewish history. A Qumran Institute was established at Groningen in 1961 by Adam van der Woude to study the documents that became known as The Dead Sea Scrolls. Groningen supervised the publication of the material from 'the Dutch cave' (number eleven). The Qumran Institute is now part of the Faculty of Theology and Religious Studies.

MIDDLE EASTERN STUDIES

The study of the Ancient Near East has a long history at Groningen, once embracing the study of Hebrew, Aramaic, Arabic, Sumerian and Akkadian. This tradition is now represented by the Department of Middle Eastern Studies in the Faculty of Arts whose focus is on the contemporary Middle East in its historical and linguistic context. The department's research profile has a chronological span from Late Antiquity to the Muslim Brotherhood and Islamic State.

and staff, the importance of English for publishing research and the increased employability of Dutch students. It also stated that international staff and students should have easy access to free Dutch language lessons. By 2017, out of 167 master-level programmes, 126 were taught in English as were 29 of the 48 bachelor-level degrees. However, the university as a whole has not switched from Dutch and the English question is part of a debate that is taking place in all Dutch universities as well as in parliament.

For some time, there have been several voices raised against universal English adoption. In 2005 the Heymans Chair of the History of Psychology, Douwe Draaisma, warned that if European higher education was delivered in English it would entail a reliance on English-language textbooks and research which would negatively affect variety among universities, precisely the opposite of what individual research institutes aim for. Although Draaisma affirmed the need for and usefulness of English programmes at some faculties, he strenuously opposed the introduction of all-English programmes in others, arguing that this would not make them more international, but merely anglophone.

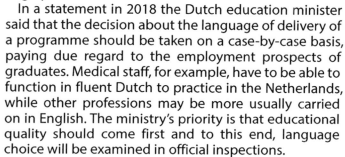

In a statement in 2018 the Dutch education minister said that the decision about the language of delivery of a programme should be taken on a case-by-case basis, paying due regard to the employment prospects of graduates. Medical staff, for example, have to be able to function in fluent Dutch to practice in the Netherlands, while other professions may be more usually carried on in English. The ministry's priority is that educational quality should come first and to this end, language choice will be examined in official inspections.

In The Netherlands, near universal teaching in English would entail considerable practical difficulties. In 2001, the university newspaper reported that many Dutch students had problems writing papers in English and it is not clear how things could have changed substantially since then. Graduates from secondary school often have a limited proficiency level (upper intermediate at best), which is insufficient to read complicated research articles and understand intricate matters in course books written in a foreign language. As the English language level of Dutch students is comparatively high, the same observation applies to many international students. (It is always a little complicated to judge what a given result in English in any assessment system means, even when the Common European Framework of Reference for Language (CEFR) is used.) The abilities of native speakers of a language cannot be taken for granted. Native speakers of English do not, at the age of 18 or 19, naturally read and write in a manner appropriate to higher education. In examinations at the Department of English, some of them fail due to the standard of their communication. In English-speaking countries English language skills are often taught at university level. Similarly, native speakers of Dutch do not always emerge from school with the language level required for jobs in the Netherlands. A scenario where many graduates can neither communicate in English nor in Dutch at degree level is presumably one that is too dysfunctional to contemplate.

In an English-language institution many, but not all, employees would have to have a high language standard (important staff from the chief accountant to the cleaners could be unaffected). Support staff, who design forms, write regulations and minute meetings, were not hired after tests of their English and bringing them all up to the required standard would be a lengthy and expensive procedure. More importantly though, students have continuously pointed out that the English skills of some lecturers are insufficient for teaching, which has a predictably negative effect on the quality of education. This was noted by the minister of education in 2018. The Groningen *Language and Culture Policy* recommended that the quality of teaching might be monitored using 'the observation/assessment of real teaching events ... based on video evidence'. An assessment of actual teaching by a centralised body would ensure that English-language programmes were good across the institution. As yet, while the number of programmes taught in English increases, such universal testing of English has not been implemented.

Gobbledygook

Regardless of the language in question, a feature of university life in the last decade is the prevalence of gobbledygook. This is not unique to Groningen or to Dutch universities. The English-language discourses surrounding higher-education are saturated with 'excellent', 'world-class', 'cutting edge', 'future-proof' objects and people. This inflation leads to a jadedness when confronted by things which are indeed world class. At Groningen, this inflation might be traceable to the increased commercialisation remarked in Chapter 11. Rather than the language of science or even clear communication, the language of advertising has come to the fore. The University or Faculty Board that would try and roll this back and state that some things are only 'quite good' or 'satisfactory' would presumably be replaced for failing to meet the demands of the age. The evidence is that if someone keeps repeating something that it will be taken to be true. On the other hand, in the last century, the question of the responsibility of universities to their own values has been raised in various forms.

An important feature of the modern history of universities is the extension of Gobbledygook to the filing of non-significant statistics and the existence of processes which do not extend beyond paper (so that various qualitative reports can be drawn up). Part of this has been imposed on Groningen by external bodies such as the ministry for education who need to generate numbers for slippery but very important things such as calculation of added value or research worth. Nudity on Dutch campuses is discouraged, unless you are an emperor.

Four Centuries, 2014

Hearing about parties that you were not at is more often tedious than engaging. Despite this, something must be said about the celebration of the university's quatercentenary. For one thing, it was the largest commemoration in the institution's history. For another, unlike any previous anniversary, this one left text, images and video that is easily accessible on the internet. This ranges from personal photos to a short-university movie, *For Infinity* (Sjaan&Nout, dir.). The latter took its title from the official designation of the celebration, a visual pun on 400 and 4∞ (four infinity) which proved irresistible even though it was both hubristic and impossible (see Gobbledygook above). However, this did not detract from an extraordinary and varied occasion.

The festivities took two years of planning, which is unsurprising for a series of events that attracted 150,000 people. There was a range of performances (including a musical about Aletta Jacobs) and sports events (notably a boat race with students from the old foe, Münster). Public lectures were delivered by important scholars such as the French anthropologist Dr Bruno Latour and the British Astronomer Royal, Martin, Baron Rees. Ten honorary doctorates were conferred. Exhibitions dealt with four centuries of student life (at the Groningen Museum) and 400 years of science (at the A-Kerk). As the numbers who attended suggest, it was not a jamboree restricted to the university and a few guests – it was pitched as a civic and provincial celebration of the 'university of the North'. As such, there were events for children and events that took place in towns throughout the region. On 15 May, King Willem-Alexander made an official visit and delivered a pithy speech. The rector, Elmer Sterken, outlined his vision of the university as a place where 'young, talented students, supervised by experienced academics, are primed for their role in society'.

Eleven Faculties

The number of Groningen's faculties has expanded from its original four to eleven. Two of these have only recently been founded: University College Groningen (2014) and Campus Fryslân (2018).

Arts | Letteren: The first Arts professor was appointed in 1811. Now based in the Harmony Building in the city centre, the faculty has 5,000 students and 700 staff. It has a wide variety of departments dealing with literature, language, linguistics, culture, history, media studies and international relations. The departments of English and of American studies teach solely in English. Classics continues a Latin and Greek tradition that goes back to the foundation of the university. Students of Arctic and Antarctic studies have demanding field assignments. Specialist postgraduate programmes include Euroculture and international humanitarian action. The faculty is the location of a thriving Language Centre which teaches short courses in Arabic, Dutch, German, Hebrew, Italian, Portuguese, Russian and Spanish. It offers a free massive open online course (MOOC) which is an introduction to Dutch: <www.rug.nl/language-centre/e-learning/online-dutch/introduction-to-dutch-mooc>.

Behavioural & Social Sciences | Gedrags- en Maatschappijwetenschappen: The faculty's first professor was appointed in 1964. It includes the departments of psychology (e.g. clinical, forensic, neuropsychology), sociology and education (for teachers and for special educational needs). Many psychology courses are delivered in English (including the two-year research master) and the faculty has a high proportion of international students. Because of the numbers of applicants, entry to the BA has been selective (the current details of the procedure are always online).

Campus Fryslân: This is the newest faculty of the university, having begun degree-level courses in 2018. It is based in Leeuwarden, the main city of the province of Friesland. The campus is the home of University College Fryslân which offers three year BA degrees and postgraduate programmes including global responsibility and leadership, sustainable entrepreneurship, multilingualism and tourism geography. Its first dean, Prof. Jouke de Vries, was selected as president of the university in June 2018.

Economics & Business (FEB) | Economie en Bedrijfskunde: Its first professor was appointed in 1948. Specialised research areas include public health, inequality, digital business models, orgazational resilience, and creativity. It is based in the Duisenberg Building at Zernike which is named after one of its most notable alumni, Wim Duisenberg (1935–2005), president of the central bank of the Netherlands and then of the European central bank. Klaas Knot, the current president of the Dutch central bank is both a Groningen graduate and an honorary professor.

Law | Rechtsgeleerdheid: Founded in 1614, it is of the largest Law faculties in the

The Old Hortus (Department of Psychology)

Netherlands. It is currently based in the Harmony building. Its programme in International and European law is taught in English. Distinguished alumni include Dirk Stikker (1897–1979), who was variously a Dutch minister for foreign affairs, the director of Heineken, and secretary general of NATO.

MEDICAL SCIENCES | MEDISCHE WETENSCHAPPEN: Working with the UMCG, the faculty was established with the university in 1614 (see chapter 6). Its departments include dentistry and movement sciences as well as medicine.

PHILOSOPHY | WIJSBEGEERTE: Founded in 1614, it is based in the city centre. The faculty has about 450 students and focuses on the philosophy of science, ethics, political philosophy, the philosophy of mind, and the history of philosophy. Several of its postgraduate courses are taught in English.

SCIENCE & ENGINEERING (FSE): Formerly the Faculty of Mathematics and Natural Sciences (*Wiskunde en Natuurwetenschappen*), it has abandoned any Dutch title. Its first professor was appointed in 1815. It is based at the Zernike Campus north west of the city centre. As well as the traditional sciences of astronomy, physics, chemistry and biology, the faculty houses computing science, environmental science, nanoscience and pharmacy. The KVI-Centre for Advanced Radiation Technology works on subatomic particles. Most of the faculty's teaching is done in English.

SPATIAL SCIENCES | RUIMTELIJKE WETENSCHAPPEN: The roots of the discipline in Groningen go back to 1948 when Hendrik Jacob Keuning was appointed professor of economic and human geography. The first professor of spatial science was appointed in 1987. It is the only independent Faculty of Spatial Sciences in the Netherlands and includes the study of economic geography, urban planning, tourism, population studies, water and coastal management (vital in a national context) and real estate studies. Several courses are offered jointly with international partners.

THEOLOGY AND RELIGIOUS STUDIES | GODGELEERDHEID EN GODSDIENSTWETENSCHAP: A founding faculty of the university, its students can now study Buddhism, Islam and Hinduism alongside Judaism and Christianity, developing their interests in history, culture and anthropology. Staff study the sanctification of Michael Jackson, Coptic, the Dead Sea Scrolls and Indian religions. The BA in religious studies is wholly taught in English, as are several MA programmes. The university is also the home of part of the Protestant Theological University which has an MA in Protestant theology that is taught in English.

UNIVERSITY COLLEGE GRONINGEN: Established in 2014, it teaches a curriculum in English with three tracks, humanities, science and social science. It is unusual in Groningen as it is residential in its first year. Of the 120 students admitted annually, roughly 40% of the students are from the Netherlands and 60% are from abroad.

CRYSTAL BALLS

The university projects that student numbers will increase to 35,000 by 2025. Currently, it is not envisaged that numbers would grow much beyond this. To cater for this, construction is underway, but it will still be challenging to keep up with expansion. The building plan anticipates that 'future growth will probably be confined to certain sectors (including green and technology), and an increasing influx of international students'. As a result, it will not be necessary to extend every part of the university. As well as more space, the plans emphasize the quality of that space. For example, the Zernike Campus is to incorporate 'a lively, open green park'. Facilities of faculties that are scattered in different locations will be grouped to form communities in which 'students are encouraged to spend more time in their own faculty, surrounded by like-minded students as well as lecturers'. In part this will be to counteract the enormous size of the institution as a whole.

As well as teaching buildings, student accommodation has to be addressed. At the beginning of 2018–19 some students were even living in tents. The question is complicated by the fact that the university cannot easily cap the numbers admitted to courses and there is no university-owned accommodation. Groningen does co-operate with housing corporations and the municipal authorities to facilitate placing students (especially international ones), but this does not abolish the necessity to begin searching for accommodation as early as possible.

The current strategic plan for 2015–24 has several goals in different areas. Some of the very concrete ones include:

- expecting students to become responsible partners in their learning;
- putting knowledge to use in economic and social processes;
- fostering an innovative and entrepreneurial attitude;
- engagement with the needs of the northern Netherlands;
- more involvement with alumni.

Forecasts do not include a merger with the Hanzehogeschool, although that might surely appeal to some governments on the grounds of synergy if nothing else. It could well be that 60,000 students are required to survive in the sector by 2030.

In the light of the university's history with its succession of changes and its highs and lows it is impossible and foolish to say much beyond this. Even the 2015–24 plan has been overtaken by events as the Yantai campus (which was included in the first point on the plan's list of ambitions) has not materialised. Just as in the past, the rumble of international political instability can end up having far-reaching effects in Groningen. The rate of technological change, unparalleled since 1614, is such that it defeats any long-term predictions and managements might sometimes usefully turn to science fiction.

During the celebrations of the university's four hundredth anniversary the rector, Elmer Sterken, had special licence to muse on what the place would be like in 2064. It was, he stressed, 'a best guess'. He predicted that 'student mobility will return to the seventeenth-century Dutch level and ... Groningen will be part of an international network with different campuses across the globe'. In stating that 'students will need more capabilities to judge the value of information instead of acquiring knowledge alone', he was on safe ground as he rightly regards this as a skill that is immediately relevant. In the light of the university's history, he had a wish: 'I truly hope that our children can enjoy academic education in freedom'. The children may not be 'ours' as they might be international ones and perhaps some might conceivably live valuable lives without having any offspring, but the rector's wish was surely endorsed by the majority of the members of the university present. The challenge will be to see this freedom realised.

APPENDIX I

DUTCH UNIVERSITIES

University	English Name	Founded	Students
Erasmus Universiteit (Rotterdam)	Erasmus University	1913	28,000
Maastricht University	Maastricht University	1976	16,300
Radboud Universiteit (Nijmegen)	Radboud University	1923	21,000
Rijksuniversiteit Groningen	University of Groningen	1614	31,000
Technische Universiteit Eindhoven	Eindhoven University of Technology	1956	12,300
Tilburg University	Tilburg University	1927	13,000
TU Delft	Delft University of Technology	1842	23,400
Universiteit Leiden	University of Leiden	1575	28,100
Universiteit Twente	University of Twente	1961	10,000
Universiteit Utrecht	University of Utrecht	1636	32,000
Universiteit van Amsterdam (UvA)	University of Amsterdam	1632	30,000
Vrije Universiteit Amsterdam	VU	1880	23,000
Wageningen University	Wageningen University	1876	12,000

Other Universities
Open Universiteit, nationwide.
Protestantse Theologische Universiteit (PThU), Groningen and Amsterdam
Theologische Universiteit Kampen (TU Kampen)
Theologische Universiteit Apeldoorn (TUA)
Universiteit voor Humanistiek (UVH), Utrecht

Universities of Professional Education (HBOs)
As their name suggests, these forty-three institutions offer degree programmes in the transfer of knowledge for professional practice. Not all HBOs use terms such as 'university of professional education' or 'university of applied science' in their titles and some have degrees in the practical arts (e.g. dance, musical performance, fine art). They also train many schoolteachers. HBOs are limited to awarding bachelor (four-year) and master (one or two-year) degrees. They can be very large institutions (35,000+ students). The umbrella organization for HBOs is *Vereniging Hogescholen.*

TERMINOLOGY

1-10: Dutch grading is on a 1–10 scale. There are official equivalences for this established by various foreign university systems. Approximately, 1–5 is usually a fail, 6 is a pass, 7 is an honours grade and 8–10 is an excellent mark. 10s are very rare outside the exact sciences.

academic year: currently broken into two semesters. The first begins sometime near the start of September and ends the following January. The second runs from February until the first or second week of July.

ACLO: sports organisation of the university and the *Hanzehogeschool*.

arbo-arts: occupational health doctor who assesses your fitness to work.

BAC: appointment committee. It is not a standing committee: one is formed for each appointment.

bachelor: three-year study programme equal to 180 ECTS. Only *numerus fixus* programmes have selection. The title of bachelor is protected by law.

bedrijfsarts: see *arbo-arts*.

Bommen Berend: 28 August holiday. It celebrates the defeat of the bishop of Münster who laid siege to Groningen in the seventeenth century.

BKO: see UTQ.

block: half a semester (usually 10 weeks). Includes examination time.

Broerstraat 5: alumni magazine of RUG.

BSA: Binding Study Advice. Orwellian term for an instruction (not advice) to a student who has not passed enough courses to discontinue a degree.

BSZ: office dealing with student registration and grades.

bull: degree certificate.

CAO NU: *Collective Labour Agreement of Dutch Universities.*

Comenius Programme: Part of the NRO. It focuses on the quality of teaching in higher education and awards fellowships for projects that might improve this.

committee of deans: the deans of the university's faculties advise the rector who chairs the committee.

CROHO: *Centraal Register Opleidingen Hoger Onderwijs*, the Central Register of Higher Education Study Programmes, lists all accredited degree programmes in the Netherlands.

conclave: body that chooses the *rector magnificus*.

cum laude: Latin for 'with praise'. For a PhD, this can only be awarded when, in a written ballot of the examining committee, there are no dissenters.

daily supervisor(s): the day-to-day supervisors of a PhD student.

dean: head of a Faculty Board (but not its 'managing director' q.v.).

decan: Dutch word for 'dean' which may refer to the office of student support as well as the dean of a faculty.

docent: a lecturer without research time.

doctorate: usually a four-year programme based on independent research.

dr. (lower-case): in Dutch, this title precedes the name of a holder of a doctorate. It can be added to other titles, e.g. 'prof. dr. M. Verspoor'. Commonly and incorrectly retained in English translations.

eindexamen: exams taken at the end of a Dutch student's secondary education. Based on these, a student with a VWO curriculum can choose to study at research university.

faction: members of the University Council represent different factions (which in this case simply means interest groups and does not have the negative connotations that 'faction' often has).

Faculty Board: the executive board of a faculty, composed of the dean, the vice-dean, the managing director (i.e. finance officer), a student representative and its secretary.

Faculty Council: elected committee that advises its Faculty Board.

gown: see toga. Dutch universities do not use gowns for their graduates.

HAVO: general secondary education which is a route to a course in a HBO.

HBO (hogeschool): university of applied sciences.

Holland: North Holland and South Holland are provinces, and only provinces, of The Netherlands.

honorary doctorate: the university does not confer many honorary doctorates, usually no more than a couple in a year.

Honours College: undergraduate and postgraduate programmes offered to outstanding students in addition to their main programmes.

hora finita: the words pronounced at the end of the questioning in a PhD ceremony (*promotie*). This is exactly 45 minutes from the opening of the ceremony. People stop speaking in mid-sentence.

Hora Finita: online registration system for Groningen PhD students.

holidays: 25 and 26 December (Christmas), Good Friday, Easter Monday, 27 April (King's Day), 5 May (Liberation Day), Ascension Thursday, and Pentecost Monday.

*ius promovendi***:** The right to act as the primary supervisor of a PhD thesis. This is restricted to full professors and designated UHDs.

KNAW: *Koninklijke Nederlandse Akademie van Wetenschappen*, the Royal Netherlands Academy of Arts and Sciences. Established in 1808, membership of the academy is a mark of academic distinction.

laudatio: speech in praise of a student usually delivered by a thesis supervisor.

managing director: a confusing term sometimes used to designate the finance officer of a Faculty Board. It may have arisen due to the currency of corporate speak in universities.

master: usually a one-year (60 ECTS), but sometimes a two-year programme (120 ECTS), or a three-year programme in medical, dentistry and veterinary science. For most programmes there is no selection and graduates with a relevant bachelor's degree must be accepted. The title of master is protected by law.

MBO: secondary vocational education. Students who have completed its highest level can enter a HBO course.

mr.: title preceding the names of both male and female lawyers, e.g. 'mr. Henck Rein Umooizo'.

mutation: a term used by HR for changes in working conditions. These can be painful.

NRO: The Netherlands Initiative for Education Research is part of the NWO. It is involved in improving education at school and university levels.

NSE: *Nationale Studenten Enquête*, the independent national student survey of higher education courses. The results are available at: <www.studiekeuze123.nl>.

numerus fixus or ***numerus clausus***: a degree programme with a capped number of new students (e.g. medicine and dentistry at Groningen). Most Dutch programmes do not have such a cap.

Nuffic: *De Nederlandse Organisatie voor Internationalisering in Onderwijs*, the Dutch organization for internationalisation in education. It reports on matters affecting international students.

NVAO: The *Nederlands-Vlaamse Accreditatie Organisatie* (Netherlands-Flemish Accreditation Organization) is responsible for degrees in Dutch and Flemish universities. Its reports are online.

Window, Academy Building

NWO: The *Nederlandse Organisatie voor Wetenschappelijk Onderzoek* (The Netherlands Organisation for Scientific Research) supports and funds university research in all disciplines. It has four sections: sciences; applied and engineering sciences; social sciences and humanities; medical sciences. Three of its most important grants are named *Veni*, *Vidi* and *Vici*.

OC: see Programme Committee.

opponent: a member of the committee that questions a doctoral candidate at a *promotie*. Professors are addressed as 'highly learned opponents' and others are 'very learned opponents'.

OWI: *onderwijsinstituut*, a faculty institute for education that supervises teaching quality.

paranimf: the two paranymphs are friends of a doctoral candidate who arrange some of the celebrations associated with a *promotie*.

Programme Committee: Elected staff-student body that oversees syllabuses and teaching quality.

proefschrift: doctoral thesis.

professor: the holder of the chair of a subject .

promotie: a public PhD ceremony, sometimes misleadingly called a 'defence' (a committee might decide to award a *cum laude*, but it is not supposed to fail a thesis that has got this far). Ceremonies are usually in Dutch but it is not unusual for them to be conducted in English.

promotor: a professor who is actually or nominally supervising a PhD thesis. Every PhD student must have a *promotor*. They may have daily supervisors doing the hands-on work.

prof.: always lower-case. Precedes a professor's name in Dutch and is added to other titles, e.g. 'prof. dr. I. Visser'. Commonly and incorrectly used in English translation.

recidivist: a student repeating a course.

research master: a two-year degree (120 ECTS) designed as a preparation for doctoral study. It is not a requirement for admission to a PhD.

scientific: often incorrectly used a synonym for 'research' rather than as a reference to the natural sciences.

scriptie: undergraduate or master thesis.

secondary education: post-primary school study is streamed for students who are intended to go on to vocational, HBO, or university courses. The final exams are national ones.

Supervisory Board: governing board of the university. Members (curators), are appointed by the minister of education.

student advisor: each programme has a student advisor who helps students make decisions about their degree and who deals with personal matters. The advisor is not a member of academic staff merely stepping into a role for a brief time, but someone who has specific interest in and knowledge of student welfare.

toga: a black gown of wool and silk work by full professors in academic processions.

UB: University Library.

UD: *universitair docent*, senior lecturer, usually with tenure.

UG: now the official English abbreviation of the University of Groningen. Chosen by someone who did not see it as an expression of disgust.

UHD: *universitair hoofd docent*, the equivalent of associate professor.

UTQ: University Teaching Qualification (BKO in Dutch). Most university staff in the Netherlands have one or are about to get one (in keeping with a national agreement).

university: the term is protected by Dutch law.

University Board: composed of the president, the vice-president and the rector, it is responsible for university strategy, the development plan and budget, approving faculty regulations and supervising health and safety.

University Council: the highest elected body in the university. It is composed of twelve staff and twelve students. The council meets with the board of the university eleven times a year.

visitation: part of an ongoing cycle of inspection of the quality of Dutch universities. The visitation committee is made up of people who are not connected to the institution being examined. It ends with a public written report.

Volksuniversiteit: 'the people's university'. Over seventy such institutions exist. They provide courses in Dutch (but also in English) on a broad range of academic subjects but do not award degrees.

VSNU: *De Vereniging van Samenwerkende Universiteiten* (Association of Research Universities in the Netherlands). Established in 1985 to lobby for university interests.

VWO: secondary education for entry into a university.

WO: *wetenschappelijk onderwijs*, research-orientated education.

ILLUSTRATIONS

Photographs are by the editor unless another copyright is specified.

COVER **Front:** Window by J. Dijkstra, Aula. **Back:** *Rudolph Agricola*, anonymous eighteenth-century portrait in University Museum.

FRONT-MATTER **Contents:** *Versus* (2002) by Yland/Metz, Harmony Building. **Acknowledgements:** Mosaic, Academy Building. **Contributors:** Senate Room. **Glossary:** Tower stairs in Academy Building. **x:** *Tree of Knowledge* (1987) by Matthijs Röling and W. Muller in Aula. **xii:** Folkingestraat. **xii:** Martinikerk.

BEFORE 1614 **2:** *Beleg van Groningen, 1594* by F. Hogenberg (1596) ©Rijksmuseum **3:** *Wessel Gansfort* from *Effigies et vitae* (1654). **4:** *Rodolphus Agricola* (1940) by W. Valk, Martinikerk **7:** *Academy of Franeker* (c.1611-23) by P.F. Harlingen ©Rijksmuseum.

FOUNDATION **6:** *Ubbo Emmius*, eighteenth-century copy of 1618 portrait in University Museum. **9:** First buildings, from Fenema (1909). **10:** *Ubbo Emmius* (1909) bronze bust by B.J.W.M. van Hove in Aula. **11:** *William Macdowell*, from *Effigies et vitae* (1654). **11:** *Nicolaas Mulerius* (1614) by G. Munnintck, from *Effigies et vitae* (1654). **15:** University coat of arms. **16:** *Allegory of Victory of Gomarus over Arminius* (1618) by S. Savery, ©Rijksmuseum. **17:** Beadle's staff (1614) in University Museum.

EARLY STUDENTS **18:** A Groningen student (c. 1700) by P. Schenk ©Rijksmuseum. **20:** University seals (1685–1720), ©Rijksmuseum. **22:** Theology Faculty (2018). **25:** *Flood in Groningen, 1686* (1698) by J. Luyken (1698) ©Rijksmuseum. **27:** Christoph Bernhard von Galen, detail from *Beleg van Groningen* (1672) by the 1672 Monagrammist, ©Rijksmuseum | Carel Rabenhaupt (medal), ©Rijksmuseum. **27:** *Beleg van Groningen* (1672) by the 1672 Monagrammist.

LIBRARIES **30:** University Library (1913) by F. Wolde ©University Museum, 1992/2. **32:** Reading room of 1864 Library, from *Academia Groningana* (1914). **34:** First floor of 1864 Library, ibid. **35:** Foundation stone of University Library (1983). **36:** Plan for University Library (1990), ©University Museum, 1981/8/33. **36:** A figure of the University

of Groningen from a window (1919) by L.F. Asperslagh, in University Museum **39:** University Library in 2018.

ENLIGHTENMENT **40:** *Petrus Camper* (1781) by M.-A. Collot in Senate Room. **42:** Bernoulliborg (built 2007). **44:** *Leonard Offerhaus* (1775) by J. Houbraken, ©Rijksmuseum. **46:** Oude Boteringestraat 44 (built 1791). **47:** Beadle's staff (c. 1811), from Fenema (1909). **48:** Groningen panorama by H. Hofsnider (1743), ©Rijksmuseum. **50:** *Karl Gutzlaff* by G.C. Finden (1845) | *Pierre Janet* by E. Pirou ©Wellcome Collection, CC BY **51:** *Andrei Sacharov* (1989) by R.C. Croes, National Archives of The Netherlands. **52:** Eighteenth-century plan of Groningen (anonymous) ©Rijksmuseum.

MEDICINE **54:** *XY* (2009) by M. Borchet, UMCG. **56:** E.J. Thomassen à Thuessink by C.F.C. Bentinck, ©Rijksmuseum. **57:** Munnekholm (1786) by J. Bulthuis. **58:** Munnekeholm Hospital (1903), ©University Museum, 002977. **59:** Ten Boer (1945) by W. van der Poll, National Archives of the Netherlands. **60:** Hospital, heart operation (1954), ©University Museum, 005472. **62:** UMCG (2018).

EDUCATION ACTS **64:** Student masquerade (1859) by O. Eerlman in University Museum. **67:** Banner of the student company (1830) in Academy Building | *Peter Hofstee de Groot* by J.H. Egenberger, ©Rijksmuseum. **70:** Academy Building of 1850 by C.C.A. Last, ©Rijksmuseum. **72:** Groningen student uniform (c. 1830) by W.C. Magnenat, ©Rijksmuseum. **73:** Academy Building in 1906, ©University Museum, 006060. **74:** *Gerard Heymans* (1927) by W.J. Valk in Heymanszaal. **75:** Academy Building.

WOMEN **76:** *Aletta Jacobs* by T. van der Pant (1988). **78:** *J.R. Thorbecke* (1866) by A. Canelle, ©Rijksmuseum. **79:** *B.D.H. Tellegen* by J.H. Egenberger, ©Rijksmuseum. **81:** *Heike Kamerlingh Onnes* from Santesson (1913). **82:** Aletta Jacobs's desk in University Museum. **84:** *Jantine Tammes* (1931) in Senate Room. **85:** Model of polytope by Alicia Boole-Stott in University Museum. **86:** *C.E. Visser* in 1964, in Senate Room.

WARS **88:** Groningen in 1945, National Archives of the Netherlands. **91:** *Leonard Polak* (1973) by O.B. de Kat from a 1934 photo in Senate Room. **92:** *Fritz Zernike* (2003) by J.M.J.L. Roebrock in Senate Room. **93:** *R.W. Zandvoort* (1941) by J. Dijkstra in Senate Room. **95:** Stumbling stones in Folkingestraat. **98:** Johan Gerritsen's cell in the House of Detention, courtesy of Truus Gerritsen-Weg. **99:** Stefan Radt (2009) by M. Thomas, Michiel Thomas, <www.flickr.com/photos/25873089@ N00/3547494658>, CC BY-SA 2.0. **101 & 102:** window by J. Dijkstra in Aula. **89:** *B.V.A. Röling* (1988) by Matthijs Röling in Senate Room.

Museums **104:** Skeletons in University Museum. **106:** Anatomy Collection. **107:** University Museum collection room.

Expansion **108:** Harmony Building. **110:** Queen Juliana conferred with doctorate (1964) by J. van Bilsen, National Archives of the Netherlands. **111:** Student protest (1971), unknown photographer, National Archives of the Netherlands. **112:** *Non scholae sed vitae* by Marte Röling (1999). **115:** English students (1978), unknown photographer. **117:** Porters, Harmony Building (2018). **119:** Smitsborg (built 2002).

Millennium **121 & 123:** Nijenborgh 6 (built 2016). **122:** *Ben Feringa* (2017) by F. Broos et al. **124:** Duisenberg Building. **127:** *The Changing Same* by M. Blok and B. Lugthart (2000), Zernike Campus. **128:** View from Masada. **130:** Doctoral conferral. **133:** The Old Hortus. **134:** Linnaeusborg (built 2010).

Appendices etc. **136:** *Jan Huizing* (2018). **139:** From stained glass window, Academy Building stairwell (1909). **142:** Linnaeusborg. **146:** Bicycle garage, Zernike. **150:** Aletta Jacobs Hall with *Untitled* (1996) by H. Ovind in foreground. **154:** Academy Tower. **159:** *Hero Jan Kars* (1912) by F. van Wolde, from a photo of 1907. **142:** Tiles in Academy Building.

REFERENCES

BEFORE 1614
MacCaffrey (1992) 269–71; Israel (1995) 247–8;
van der Werff (2003) 16; Kamen (2004) 89–90.

ADUARD: *Effigies et Vitae* (1654) 1–11; Blok and
Molhuysen (1921); Hermans and Huisman
(1996) 23; Agricola (2002) 3–7, 231; Augustijn
(2003) 3, 14; Bakker (2003) 23, 26; van der
Laan (2003); van Leijenhorst (2003) 15–16;
Oberman (2003) 97, 104, 108, 113, 115, 118;
Moolenbroek (2004); Koops and Smit (2009)
13–15; Termeer and van Berkel (2009) 5–7;
Akkerman (2012) 113, 217.

FRANEKER: Israel (1995) 572–3; van Sluis (2015)
8–9, 22.

FOUNDATION
FOUNDATION: Vanderjacht (2004); von Martels
(2009) 407–9; Koops and Smit (2009) 14–17,
261.

GRONINGEN: Hermus and Voorhoeve (1989)
17; Termeer and van Berkel (2009) 8–10, 12;
Koops and Smit (2009) 14–17, 30, 261; Lokin
(2014).

BUILDINGS: Hermus and Voorhoeve (1989) 13;
Hoogendijk (1989) 7–8.

PROFESSORS: *Effigies et vitae* (1654) 12–24, 28–74;
Langeraad (1907); Loosjes (1919–31); Toomer
(1996) 98–101; Koops and Smit (2009) 263–5;
van Maanen (2004); Venning (2004); *Catalogus
professorum* (2014).

PRINTING: Koops and Smit (2009) 117.

ARMS: Vanderjacht (2004) 38; Koops and Smit
(2009) 30.

BEADLE'S STAFF: Smit (2006) 47.

EARLY STUDENTS
INTRODUCTION: Koops and Smit (2009) 263–5.

TOWN AND GOWN; BURSE: Jonckbloet (1864) 49,
51–2; Hermus and Voorhoeve (1989) 17;
Kampman (1989) 41, 45–53; Termeer and van
Berkel (2006) 18; Koops and Smit (2009) 264.

ACADEMIC LIFE: Koops and Smit (2009) 35–8, 117.

MISBEHAVIOUR: Jonckbloet (1864) 175, 233,
236–9; van der Ven (2003) 244–5; Kampman
(1989) 43–5.

ORGANIZATIONS: Kampman (1989) 53–4; van der
Ven (2003) 231.

INTERNATIONAL STUDENTS: Jonckbloet (1864) 49;
van der Ven (2003) 265–7; Life (2004); Wright
(2004); Birken (2008); Termeer and van Berkel
(2009) 13.

BOMMEN BEREND: Jonckbloet (1863) 61–73;
Termeer and van Berkel (2009) 25; Dethlefs
(2010).

LIBRARIES
GENERAL: Mulerius (1619); Roos (1914) 9, 12–13;
Hermans (1996) 51, 57; de Vries (2011);
Huisman (2014) 14, 17–18, 26, 29, 31, 35,
38–9; 61–9; *Universiteitsbibliotheek Groningen:
Renovatie,* 5–7, 13, 25, 27.

18TH & 19TH CENTURIES: Roos (1914) 17–33, 38–49.

ADDITIONS: Koops and Klaver (1987) 23–32,
39–40.

POSTMA: Boom and ten Bruggencate (1999) 67.

SPECIAL COLLECTIONS: Huisman (2014) 50, 60–1,
80.

DIGITAL COLLECTIONS: Mulerius (1619); *Digital
Collections* (2018).

BOOKS: Huisman (2014).

ENLIGHTENMENT
BERNOULLIS: Fellmann and Fleckenstein (1981)
51–6; Boom and ten Bruggencate (1999) 64;
Smit (2006) 12; Scylla (2008) 254–7.

CRISIS: Jonckbloet (1864) 99, 104, 108, 110, 112;
Smit (2009) 20–1; van Berkel (2014) 259, 429.

EEREDOCTORAAT: Sakarov (1975); Darnell (2000);
Lutz (2000) 123–5; Grant and Stern (2004);
Sherrington and Overy (2004); Carroy and
Plas (2008); Dolman (2008); Sörlin (2008); van
Berkel (2014) 280.

ORANGE-NASSAU: Jonckbloet (1864) 123, 126,
152–3, 157–8; van Berkel (2009a) 22–3.

OFFERHAUS: Jonckbloet (1864) 162; Deursen
(1957) 11–14, 19–27, 30, 32–9, 45–9; Rinzema
(1997) 21–2.

SCIENCE: Zeijlmaker (1989) 68–72; van Berkel
(1999) 76–8.

CAMPER: Kuijer (1989) 3–8; Boom and ten Bruggencate (1999) 29; Meijer (1999) 7–8, 18–20, 74–7, 179, 183–8, 190; van der Korst (2008) 99; ter Sluis (2009) 27.

BOTERINGESTRAAT 44: Boom and ten Bruggencate (1999) 31.

WAR: Jonckbloet (1864) 163–4, 169–71, 174–8, 185–9.

BONAPARTES: Caljé (2009) 118; van Berkel (2014) 403–9.

MEDICINE
INTRODUCTION: Tammeling (1978) 20, 22–3, 26–7, 30, 32–4; Termeer and van Berkel (2009) 14–15.

HOSPITALS: Tammeling (1978) 38–42, 45–53, 56, 65, 68–9, 74–5, 80–1, 85, 89, 98, 103–5, 119, 160, 256, 266–8, 279; de Wilde (1979) 48; Bolt et al. (2010); 'Body donation programme'.

ERIBA: Lansdorp and de Haan (2018) 73.

SEXY SCIENCE: Shultz et al. (1999).

UMCG: Mens (2012) 101–12; 'Het UMCG'.

EDUCATION ACTS
1815: Jensma and de Vries (1997); van Berkel (1999) 100–1; Caljé (2009) 314–7.

BELGIUM: Smit (2006) 57; Blom (2006) 395–6; Roegiers and van Sas (2006) 315–6.

DE GROOT: Blom (2006) 404–5; Bos (2010) 147–51.

STEAM: 'Prominent Professors'.

ACADEMY BUILDINGS: Smit (2006) 13–14, 15–19; Hofman (2014) 36–7.

STUDENT NUMBERS: de Wilde (1979); Caljé (2009) 114–20, 154–90; van Berkel (2014) 671.

ACTS: van Berkel (1999) 126, 128, 131; Bank and van Buuren (2004) 245–9.

SOCIAL CHANGE: Caljé (2009) 234–72.

KAPTEYN: Blaauw (1981) 235–40.

SOCIETIES: Caljé (2008); Caljé (2009) 401–23, 477–9.

HEYMANSZAAL: Heymans (1914); Boom and ten Bruggencate (1999) 37; Smit (2006) 25; Blom (2006) 419; 'Gerard Heymans'.

SENATE: Smit (2006) 51–3; *Catalogus professorum* (2014).

WOMEN
BUST: Boom and ten Bruggencate (1999) 56.

VAN SCHURMAN: Irwin (1998) 1–23.

ALETTA JACOBS: de Wilde (1979) 13–18, 21, 27, 29–33, 35–40, 43–8, 51–6, 58–60, 72–3; Feinberg (1996) 203–5; Jacobs (1996) 3–4, 7, 9, 11, 13, 16, 17, 21–24, 49, 52–3, 74, 101; de Wilde (1998) 40–84.

NOBLE DEFENDER: van Delft (2007) 55, 66, 111.

ARTS: de Wilde (1998) 134–59, 262, 269; de Wilde (2016); Blankendaal (2017).

CONTINUING DEBATE: Bolton and Brading (1992); de Wilde (1987) 40–1; Creese (2004); 'Prominent Professors'; Aletta Jacobs Prize'; 'Rosalind Franklin Fellowships'.

WARS
INTRODUCTION: Smit (2006) 37.

NEUTRAL: Stevenson (2004) 245–50; Blom (2006) 428; van Meurs (2006) 136–8; Wielinga (2014).

INTERWAR: Boiten (1980) 203–4; Blom (2006) 410; van Meurs (2006) 140.

FRITZ ZERNIKE: Baneke (2005) 40–2.

ANGLO-AMERICAN INSTITUTE: Zandvoort (1941–63); Scott-Smith (2009) 984–5; Gerritsen (2013).

WAR: Dijkstra (1979); Boiten (1980) 203; Ashworth (1995) 17–26; Foot (2001); van der Poel (2004) 132–47; Baneke (2005) 44–9; van Meurs (2006) 143; van Hasselt (2013); Beevor (2018) 378–9.

DER CLERCKE CRONIKE: Boiten (1980) 204; Raadt (2002); van Berkel (2003) 59; van Meurs (2006) 141.

HANS GERRITSEN: Visser (1964) 33–4; Henkes (1997a); Henkes (1997b); Henkes (1997c) 18–9; van Berkel (2005) 254–8, 364–5, 579–80; Bunt (2013); van der Veen (2013).

POST-WAR: Boer and Jonkman (1990) 261–2; van Berkel (2005) 411–2; van Meurs (2006) 145–7.

STEFAN RADT: 'Eredoctoraat' (2010).

ROYAL GIFT: Dijkstra (1952); Boom and ten Bruggencate (1999) 41.

POLEMOLOGICAL INSTITUTE: Verwey (1995); Cryer (2011) 120; Roelofsen (2013).

MUSEUMS
INTRODUCTION: Smit (2008) 15–16.

COLLECTIONS: 'Geschiedenis van het Universiteitsmuseum'; Le Grand (1998), 44; Inside Out (2010), 13–16; *Stichting Volkenkundige Collectie Nederland*; *Catalogus professorum* (2014); Reerink (2018).

EXPANSION
THREE COMPLEXES: Baneke (2005) 55–6, 58; van Berkel (2005) 443–4; van Meurs (2006) 147–8, 155–6; van Berkel (2009b).

STUDENTS: Henssen (1989) 398; van Berkel, and Smit (1999) 55–6; van Berkel (2005) 37, 508, 513; Baneke (2005) 74–5, 80, 93–4; van Meurs (2006) 149.

AMONG PROFESSORS: 'De Gram van Hermans'; Boom and ten Bruggencate (1999) 63.

DISHARMONY: Henssen (1989) 83–6; Goot (2015) 11.

ASSASSINATION: de Rooy (2013).

FEES: van Berkel and Smit (1999) 153.

ANGUS MADDISON: Maddison (1994); Goldman (2014).

PROGRAMMES: Henssen (1989) 167, 103, 384; van Berkel and Smit (1999) 166–9; Baneke (2005) 80–2, 94.

NESTOR: Blaauw (1999); Chavannes (2000).

MILLENNIUM
GENERAL: Kuné and Zwarts (2009) 80–3; Fransen (2010) 15; *Facts and Figures* (2017).

PROGRAMMES: Henssen (1989) 103, 167; Baneke (2005) 80–1, 93–4, 100.

CHINA: Langeler (2017); 'Branch campus Yantai'; 'Yantai in Thirteen Steps' (2018); Fu (2018), 111; Pijlman (2018); van der Berg, Leij and Sterken (2018), 12.

BSA: Blaauw (2010) 15; Zinkstok and Romanshuk (2011) 4–5.

RESEARCH: 'Sustainable Society'; 'Leading Research'; *Think Bold* (2015).

BEN FERINGA: Colstee-Wieringa (2016) 6, 8.

QUMRAN: Popovič (2018).

INTERNATIONALISATION & DIVERSITY: Lazarov (2011) 14; *Think Bold* (2015) 7; Engelshoven (2018).

ENGLISH: Henfling and Hoogendoorn (2000) 11;

Kettenis (2001) 7; Arbouw (2005) 11; Baneke (2005) 101; Kootstra (2011) 11; *Language and Culture Policy* (2014); Engelshoven (2018).

FOUR CENTURIES: Browers et al. (2014); Sjaan&Nout (2014).

COOPERATION: 'About ACLO'; Pijlman (2018).

CRYSTAL BALLS: Browers et al. (2014) 32; Van der Goot (2015) 5, 7, 15; *Think Bold* (2015); Langeler (2018) 5, 7, 15.

APPENDICES
Education System; 'Universities of applied science'.

BIBLIOGRAPHY

Abbreviations

BWN: *Biografisch Woordenboek van Nederland*, <http://resources.huygens.knaw.nl/bwn>.

DSB: C.C. Gillespie et al. eds. *Complete Dictionary of Scientific Biography*. Detroit: Charles Scribner's Sons, 2007.

ODNB: D. Cannadine, ed. *Oxford Dictionary of National Biography*, <www.oxforddnb.com>.

RUG: University of Groningen.

UB: Universiteitsbibliotheek (University Library).

Bibliography

'About ACLO'. ACLO. <www.aclosport.nl/en/about-aclo>, accessed 15 July 2018.

Academia Groningana MDCIV–MCMXIV: Gedenkboer ter Gelegenheid van het Derde Eeuwfeest der Universiteit te Groningen Uitgeven in Opdracht van den Academischen Senaat (1914). Groningen: P. Noordhoff.

'Aletta Jacobs Prize'. RUG. < www.rug.nl/about-us/where-do-we-stand/quality-works/aletta-jacobs-prize>, accessed 24 June 2018.

AGRICOLA, R. (2002). *Letters*. Ed. and trans. A. van der Laan and F. Akkerman. Assen: Van Gorcum.

AKKERMAN, F., C.G. HUISMAN AND A.J. VANDERJACHT, eds (2003). *Wessel Gansfort (1419–1489) and Northern Humanism*. Leiden: Brill.

AKKERMAN, F., ed. (2012). *Rudolph Agricola: Six Lives and Erasmus's Testimonies*. Assen: Van Gorcum.

ASHWORTH, G.J. (1995). *The City as Battlefield: The Liberation of Groningen, April 1945*. Groningen Studies 61. Groningen: Faculty of Spatial Sciences.

AUGUSTIJN, C. (2003). 'Wessel Gansfort's Rise to Celebrity'. In Akkerman, Huisman and Vanderjacht eds.

BAKKER, F.J. (2003). 'A Commemorative Mass for Wessel Gansfort'. In Akkerman, Huisman and Vanderjacht eds.

BANEKE, D.M. (2005). *De Groningse Eeuw van de Natuurwetenschappen*. Assen: Boekvorm.

BANK, J. and M. VAN BUUREN (2004). *1900: The Age of Bourgeois Culture*. Trans. L. Richards and J. Rudge. Basingstoke: Macmillan.

BEEKE, J.R. (2004). 'Comrie, Alexander'. *ODNB*.

BEEVOR, A. (2018). *Arnhem: The Battle for the Bridges, 1944*. London: Viking.

BERG, MAX VAN DER, ET AL. EDS (2018). *Passion and Performance: Liber Amicorum Sibrand Poppema*. Groningen: RUG.

BERG, MAX VAN DER, L. DE LEIJ AND E. STERKEN (2018). 'Introduction'. In van der Berg et al. eds.

BERKEL, K. VAN (1999). 'The Legacy of Stevin: A Chronological Narrative'. In K. van Berkel, A. van Helden and L. Palm eds. *A History of Science in the Netherlands: Surveys, Themes and Reference*. Brill: Leiden.

BERKEL, K. VAN (2003). 'Levend Land: Regionaal besef aan de Groningse Universiteit aan de Vooravond van de Tweede Wereldoorlog'. In M.G.J. Duivendak, ed. *Regionaal Besef in het Noorden*. Assen: Van Gorcum.

BERKEL, K. VAN (2005). *Academische Illusies: De Groningse Universiteit in een Tijd van Crisis, Bezetting en Herstel, 1930–1950*. Amsterdam: Bert Bakker.

BERKEL, K. VAN (2009a). '1749 Oranje Boven!' In Termeer and van Berkel eds.

BERKEL, K. VAN (2009b). 'Bouwen voor de expansie'. In Termeer and van Berkel eds.

BERKEL, K. VAN (2014). *Universiteit van het Noorden: Vier Eeeuwen Academisch Leven in Groningen.* Vol. 1: *De Oude Universiteit, 1614–1876.* Hilversum: Verloren.

BERKEL, K. VAN (2017). *Universiteit van het Noorden: Vier Eeeuwen Academisch Leven in Groningen.* Vol. 2: *De Klassieke Universiteit, 1876–1945.* Hilversum: Verloren.

BERKEL, K. VAN, and F.R.H. SMIT, eds (1999). *Een Universiteit in de Twintigste Eeuw.* Groningen: Rijksuniversiteitswinkel.

BIRKEN, W. (2008). 'Rand, Samuel'. *ODNB.*

BLAAUW, A. (1981). 'Kapteyn, Jacobus Cornelius'. *DSB* 7.

BLAAUW, J. (1999). 'College forceert één digitale standaard'. *UK,* 28 Oct.

BLAAUW, J. (2010). 'The party is over, folks: Rector Magnificus Frans Zwarts on education'. *UK,* 10 Dec.: 15.

BLANKENDAAL, S. (2017). 'Visser, Elizabeth.' In *Digitaal Vrouwenlexicon van Nederland.* <http://resources.huygens.knaw.nl/vrouwenlexicon/lemmata/data/VisserElizabeth>.

BLOK, P.J. and P.C. MOLHUYSEN (1921). 'Praedinius, Regnerus of Reinier Veldman'. In idem., eds, *Nieuw Nederlandsch Biografisch Woordenboek.* Vol 5. Leiden: Sijthoff.

BLOM, J.C.H. (2006). 'The Netherlands since 1830'. In J.C.H. Blom and E. Lamberts, eds. *History of the Low Countries.* New ed. Trans. J.C. Kennedy. New York: Berghahn.

'Body donation programme'. University of Groningen. <http://neuroscience.umcg.nl/en/facilities/dissection-room/body-donation-program>, accessed 1 June 2018.

BOER, J.B. DE, and W. JONKMAN (1990). *Militair Gezag in Groningen.* Assen: Van Gorcum.

BOITEN, E.A.J. (1980). 'De Groningse Universiteit'. In E.A.J. Boiten et al. *Groningen in Oorlogstijd: Aspecten van de Bezettingsjaren 1940–1950.* Groningen: Knoop & Niemeijer.

BOLT, S., E. VENBRUX, R. EISINGA, J.B.M. KUKS, J.G. VEENING and P.O. GERRITS (2010). 'Motivation for body donation to science: More than an altruistic act'. *Annals of Anatomy,* vol. 192: 70–4.

BOLTON, T.B. and A.F. BRADING (1992). 'Edith Bülbring, 27 December 1903-5 July 1990'. In *Biographical Memoirs of Fellows of the Royal Society.* <http://rsbm.royalsocietypublishing.org/content/roybiogmem/38/67>.

BOOM, E. and C. TEN BRUGGENCATE, eds (1999). *Vruchten der Verbeelding: Vier Eeuwen Kunst en Kunstzin aan de Rijksuniversiteit Groningen | Fruits of Imagination: Four Centuries of Art and Artistic Sense at the University of Groningen.* Trans. I. Sennema. Groningen: RUG.

BOS, D.J. (2010). *Servants of the Kingdom: Professionalization Among Ministers of the Nineteenth-Century Netherlands Reformed Church.* Leiden: Brill.

'Branch campus Yantai'. RUG. <www.rug.nl/about-us/internationalization/branch-campus-yantai?lang=en>, accessed 22 Jul. 2018.

BROUWERS, M., E. VAN DEN BERG and E. STERKEN (2014). *Celebrating 400 Years: University of Groningen.* Groningen: RUG.

BUNT, G. (2013). 'In Memory of Johan Gerritsen (1920–2013)'. *English Studies,* 94:6: 731–2.

CALJÉ, P.A.J. (2008). 'Studentenmaskerades in de negentiende eeuw als uniek ritueel.' *Groniek,* Nov. 2008: 276–96.

CALJÉ, P.A.J. (2009). *Student Universiteit en Samenleving: De Groningse Universiteit in de Negentiende Eeuw.* Hilversum: Verloren.

CARROY, J. and R. PLAS. 'Janet, Pierre'. *DSB* 22.

Catalogus professorum Academiae Groninganae (2014). Groningen: UB. <https://hoogleraren.ub.rug.nl>.

CHAVANNES, O. (2000). 'Zin en onzin van de elektronische eeromgeving'. *UK*, 7 Dec.

Collective Labour Agreement of Dutch Universities, 2017–19. (2018). The Hague: VSNU. <www.labouragreementuniversities.nl >.

COLSTEE-WIERINGA, F., ed. (2016). *Broerstraat 5*. 32:4.

CREESE, M.R.S. (2004). 'Boole [née Everest], Mary'. *ODNB*.

CRYER, R. (2011). 'Justice Rölling (The Netherlands)'. In Y. Tanaka, T. McCormack and G. Simpson eds. *Beyond Victor's Justice? The Tokyo War Crimes Trial Revisited*. Leiden: Martinus Nijhoff.

DARNELL, D. (2000). 'Motley, John Lothrop'. *American National Biography*. Oxford University Press. <www.anb.org>.

'De Gram van Hermans'. <www.geschiedenis24.nl/andere-tijden/afleveringen/2002-2003/Onder-professoren.html>, accessed 10 May 2011.

DELFT, D. VAN (2007). *Freezing Physics: Heike Kamerlingh Onnes and the Quest for Cold*. Trans. B. Jackson. Amsterdam: Editia KNAW.

DETHLEFS, G. (2010). 'Galen, von, Christoph Bernhard'. Das Internet-Portal zur Westfälischen Geschichte. < www.lwl.org/westfaelische-geschichte/portal/Internet/finde/langDatensatz.php?urlID=537&url_tabelle=tab_person>

DEURSEN, A.T. VAN (1957). *Leonard Offerhaus: Professor Historiarum Groninganus, 1699–1779*. Groningen: J.B. Wolters.

Digital Collections, University of Groningen (2018). RUG. <http://facsimile.ub.rug.nl/cdm/>.

DIJKSTRA, A. (1979). *Professor J.M.N. Kapteyn: Ideologische Speerpunt van de SS als Rector-Magnificus aan de Rijksuniversiteit Groningen en als Voorzitter van de Stichting Saxo-Frisia*. Groningen: s.n.

DIJKSTRA, J. (1952). *The Stained Glass Windows in the Great Hall of the University of Groningen*. Groningen: De Waal.

DOLMAN, C.E. (2008). 'Koch, Heinrich Hermann Robert'. *DSB* 7.

Education System, The Netherlands: The Dutch Education System Described (2015). 2nd ed. Ver. 4. The Hague: Nuffic.

Effigies et vitae professorum Academiae Groningae et Omlandiae (1654). Groningen: J. Nicolai.

ENGELSHOVEN, I. VAN (2018). 'Internationalisering in evenwicht'. Ministerie van Onderwijs, Cultuur en Wetenschap. Ministerial letter to parliament. 4 Jun.

'Eredoctoraat voor Stefan Radt'. RUG, 2010. <www.rug.nl/news/2010/01/20091130_eredoctoraat_radt>, accessed 1 Jul. 2018.

ELAUT, L. (1959). 'Nicholaus Mulerius uit Brugge, de eerst medische hoogleraar te Groningen (1564–1630)'. *Scientarium Historia*, 1:1: 3–13.

Facts and Figures (2017). Groningen: RUG.

FEINBERG, H. (1996). 'Patterns of Remembrance: A Literary Afterword.' In Jacobs.

FELLMANN, E.A. and J.O. FLECKENSTEIN (1981). 'Bernoulli, Johann (Jean) I'. *DSB* 2.

FENEMA, C.H. VAN (1909). *Het Academie-Gebouw te Groningen, 1604–1909*. Groningen: Scholtens & Zoon.

FOOT, M.R.D. (2001). 'Netherlands.' In I.C.B. Dear. *The Oxford Companion to World War II*. Oxford: Oxford University Press.

FRANSEN, R. (2010). 'Big money, tiny subject: Andreas Hermann on the secret of his success'. *UK*, 25 Feb.: 15.

F<small>U</small>, Z. (2018). 'A great educator and administrator'. In van der Berg et al. eds.

'Gerard Heymans'. Royal Library. <www.kb.nl/themas/filosofie/gerard-heymans>, accessed 12 June 2018.

G<small>ERRITSEN</small> J. (2013). 'Zandvoort, Reinard Willem (1894-1990)'. *BWN* 5.

'Geschiedenis'. <www.keiweek.nl/site/kei-week/geschiedenis>, accessed 15 May 2011.

'Geschiedenis van het Universiteitsmuseum'. RUG. Expired webpage, originally accessed 15 May 2011.

G<small>OLDMAN</small>, L. (2014). 'Maddison, Angus'. *ODNB*.

G<small>OOT</small>, E. <small>VAN DER</small> (2015). *Smart Work, Smart Buildings: Accommodation Plan 2015–2024*. Groningen: RUG.

G<small>RAAF</small>, A. <small>DE</small> (1964). *De Geheele Mathesis of Wiskonst, Herstelt in Zijn Natuurlijke Gedaante*. Amsterdam: J. ten Hoorn.

G<small>RANT</small>, W.L. and R.T. S<small>TERN</small> (2004). 'Peterson, Sir William'. *ODNB*.

H<small>ASSELT</small>, L.H. <small>VAN</small> (2013). 'Kapteijn, Johannes Marie Neele (1870-1949)'. *BWN* 5.

H<small>ENFLING</small>, M. and I. H<small>OOGENDOORN</small> (2000). 'De opmars van het camping-Engels'. *UK*, 3 Feb.: 11.

H<small>ENKES</small>, B. (1997a). 'Report of conversation with J. Gerritsen'. Manuscript.

H<small>ENKES</small>, B. (1997b) 'Letter from Johan Gerritsen, 09-09-1997'. Manuscript.

H<small>ENKES</small>, B. (1997c). *Voor een 'Waarlijk Eigen Stijl': Continuïteit en Breuk Binnen een Academische Gemeenschap, Groningen 1930–1950*. Groningen: RUG.

H<small>ENSSEN</small>, E.W.A. (1989). *Rijksuniversiteit Groningen, 1964–1989*. Groningen: Wolters-Noordhoff.

H<small>ERMANS</small>, J.M.M. and G.C. H<small>UISMAN</small> (1996). *Aan de Ketting: Boek en Bibliotheek in Groningen voor 1699*. Groningen: UB.

H<small>ERMUS</small>, J. and M. V<small>OORHOEVE</small> (1989). *Het Academiegebouw: Hart van de Universiteit*. Groningen: Stichting Vrienden van de Stad Groningen.

'Het UMCG'. RUG. <www.umcg.nl/NL/UMCG/overhetumcg/Paginas/default.aspx>, accessed 28 Jun. 2018.

H<small>EYMANS</small>, G. (1914). *To the Citizens of the Belligerent States*. N.p.: Dutch Committee of the European Federation.

H<small>OFMAN</small>, B. (2014). *400 Jaar Universiteit-Groningen: Van 1614 tot 2014*. Assen: Boekvorm.

H<small>OOGENDIJK</small>, M. (1989). *Langs de Universiteit: Een Wandeling Langs 375 Jaar Universiteit*. Groningen: Regio Project.

H<small>UUSSEN</small>, A.H., ed. (2003). *Onderwijs en Onderzoek. Studie en Wetenschap aan de Academie van Groningen in de 17e en 18e Eeuw*. Hilversum: Verloren.

H<small>UISMAN</small>, G.C. (2014). *The University Library of Groningen: Four Hundred Years of History in Four Buildings, Forty Collections and Infinite Pictures*. Groningen: Barkhuis & University Library.

'Introduction to Dutch'. University of Groningen Language Centre MOOC. <www.rug.nl/language-centre/e-learning/online-dutch/introduction-to-dutch-mooc>.

Inside Out: The Human Body Dissected (2010). Groningen: RUG

I<small>SRAEL</small>, J.I. (1995). *The Dutch Republic: Its Rise, Greatness, and Fall, 1477–1860*. Oxford: Clarendon Press.

I<small>RWIN</small>, J.L. (1998). 'Introduction: Anna Maria van Schurman and Her Intellectual Circle'. In Anna Maria van Schurman. *Whether a Christian Woman Should be Educated and Other Writings from her Intellectual Circle*. Ed. J.L. Irwin. Chicago: University of Chicago Press.

JACOBS, A. (1996). *Memories: My Life as an International Leader in Health, Suffrage, and Peace*. Ed. H. Feinberg. Trans. A Wright. New York: CUNY Press.

JANSSEN, F.A. and W. OTTESPEER (2011). 'Korte Biografie van Willem Frederik Hermans'. <www.willemfrederikhermans.nl/biografie.php>, accessed 15 April 2011.

JENSMA, G. and H. DE VRIES (1997). *Veranderingen in het hoger onderwijs in Nederland tussen 1815 en 1940*. Hilversum: Uitgeverij Verloren.

JONCKBLOET, W.J.A. (1864). *Gedenkboek der Hoogeschool te Groningen, ter Gelegenheid van Haar Vijfde Halve Eeuwfeest, op Last van den Akademischen Senaat*. Groningen: J.B. Wolters.

KAMEN, H. (2004). *The Duke of Alba*. New Haven: Yale University Press.

KAMPMAN, J.G. (1989). 'De Groningse student vóór 1815'. In J. Kingma, W.R.H. Koops and F.R.H. Smit, eds. *Universitair Leven in Groningen 1614–1989*. Groningen: UB.

KETTENIS, T. (2001). 'Studenten worstelen met engelstalige werkstukken'. *UK*, 1 Feb.: 7.

KOOPS, W.R.H. and C.J.J. KLAVER (1987). *Het Nieuwe Gebouw van de Universiteitsbibliotheek te Groningen*. Groningen: UB.

KOOTSTRA, R. (2011). 'Det wos it den. Ai wil sie joe!' *UK*, 7 Apr.: 11.

KORST, J.K. VAN DER (2008). *Het Rusteloze Bestaan van Dokter Petrus Camper*. Houten: Bohn Stafleu van Loghum.

KUIJJER, P.J. (1989). *Petrus Camper (1722–1789)*. Groningen: RUG.

KUNÉ, H. and F. ZWARTS (2009). 'De mondiale universiteit: Op weg naar 2014'. In Termeer and van Berkel eds.

LAAN, A. VAN DER (2003). 'Humanism in the Low Countries before Erasmus: Rudolphus Agricola's Address to the Clergy at Worms'. In Z. von Martels and V.M. Schmidt, eds. *Antiquity Renewed: Late Classical and Early Modern Themes*. Leuven: Peeters.

LANGELER, T. (2017). 'Even if it were North Korea'. *UK*, 12 Dec.

LANGELER, T. (2018). 'Concerns about RUG's record growth'. *UK*, 26 Jun.

LANGERAAD, H.V. and H. VISSCHER (1919–31). 'Alting (Hendrik)'. In L.A. van Langeraad and H. Visscher, eds. *Het Protestantsche Vaderland: Biographisch Woordenboek van Protestantsche Godgeleerden in Nederland*. Vol. 1. Utrecht: Kemink & Zoon.

Language and Culture Policy (2015). Groningen: RUG.

LANSDORP, P. AND G. DE HAAN (2018). 'ERIBA'. In van der Berg et al. eds.

LAZAROV, T. (2011). 'Rector: 'It has to happen on its own'. *UK*, 24 Mar.: 15.

'Leading research'. RUG. <www.rug.nl/research/sustainable-society>, accessed 13 Jul. 2018.

LE GRAND, J. (1998). *Anatomisch Museum*. Groningen: RUG.

LEIJENHORST, C.G. VAN (2003). 'Rudolphus Agricola of Baflo'. In P.G. Bietenholz and T.B. Deutscher, eds. *Contemporaries of Erasmus: A Biographical Register of the Renaissance and Reformation*. 1 vol. ed. Toronto: University of Toronto Press.

LIFE, P. (2004). 'Bythner, Victorinus'. *ODNB*.

LOKIN, J.H.A. (2014). 'De oprichting van de Groninger Faculteit der Rechtsgeleerdheid'. *Rechtsgeschiedenis*. RUG <www.rjhbrink.eu/Berolini/400-jaar.htm>.

LOOSJES, J. (1919–31). 'Gomarus (Franciscus) of François Gomaer'. In J.P. de Bie and J. Loosjes, eds. *Biographisch Woordenboek van Protestantsche Godgeleerden in Nederland*. Vol. 3. s'-Gravenhage: Martinus Nijhoff.

LUTZ, J.G. (2000). 'The Legacy of Karl Friedrich August Gützlaff'. *International Bulletin of Missionary Research*, 24:3: 123–8.

MAANEN, J. VAN (2004). 'Pasor, Matthias'. *ODNB*.

MACCAFFREY, W.T. (1992). *Elizabeth I: War and Politics, 1588–1603*. Princeton: Princeton University Press.

MADDISON, A. (1994). 'Confessions of a Chiffrephile'. *Banca Nazionale del Lavoro Quarterly Review*, vol. 189.

MARTELS, Z. VON (2009). 'Ubbo Emmius, the Eternal Edict and the Academy of Groningen'. In A.A. MacDonald, Z.R.W.M. von Martels and J.R. Veenstra, eds. *Christian Humanism: Essays in Honour of Arjo Vanderjagt*. Leiden: Brill.

MEER, E. VAN DER (2011). 'Wisseling van de macht'. *Dagblad van het Noorden*, 19 Feb.: 36.

MEIJER, M.C. (1999). *Race and Aesthetics in the Anthropology of Petrus Camper, 1722–1789*. Amsterdam: Rodopi.

MEIJERS, M.R. (1993). *Verzamelen: Van Rariteitenkabinet tot Kunstmuseum*. Houten: Gaade.

MENS, N. (2012). *City Within a City: The Architecture and Building History of the University Medical Centre (UMCG)*. Trans. J. Kirkpatrick. Groningen: UMCG.

MEURS, M. VAN (2006). *Een Beeld van een Provincie*. Assen: Van Gorcum.

MOOLENBROEK, J. VAN (2004). 'Wessel Gansfort as a Teacher at the Cistercian Abbey of Aduard. The Dismissal of Caesarius of Heisterbach's *Dialogus miraculorum*'. In K. Goudriaan, J. van Moolenbroiek and A. Tervoort, eds. *Education and Learning in the Netherlands, 1400–1600*. Leiden: Brill.

MULERIUS, N. (1619). *Syllabus librorum omnium in bibliotheca Academica Groningæ & Omlandiæ* (1619). Groningen: University Library. <http://syllabus.ub.rug.nl/english/index.html>.

NAAIJER, J. (2009). 'De Koninklijke Ritzen Koeriers'. In Termeer and van Berkel eds.

OBERMAN, H.J. (2003). 'Wessel Gansforth: *Magister Contradictionis*'. In Akkerman, Huisman and Vanderjacht eds.

PARÉ, A. (1636). *De Chirurgie, Ende Alle de Opera, Ofte Wercken*. Amsterdam: C. van Breugel.

PIJLMAN, H. (2018). 'Share your talent, move the world'. In van der Berg et al. eds.

POEL, S. VAN DER (2004). *Joodse Stadjers: De Joodse Gemeenschap in de Stad Groningen, 1796–1945*. Groningen Historische Reeks 26. Assen: Van Gorcum.

POPOVIČ, M. (2018). 'Raiders of the Lost Scrolls.' In van der Berg et al. eds.

'Prominent Professors'. RUG. <www.rug.nl/society-business/university-museum/prominent-professors>, accessed 1 Jun. 2018.

RAADT, M. DE (2002). 'De Afwachtende Houding van Der Clercke'. UK, 10 Jan.: 9.

REERINK, H., ed. (2018). 'Academische Collecties'. Amsterdam: UvA, <www.academischecollecties.nl>.

RINZEMA, A.J. (1997). 'Groninger hoogleraren uit de periode 1614–1876 en hun belangstelling voor de geschiedenis der middeleeuwen'. In C. Santing ed. *De Geschiedenis van de Middeleeuwen aan de Groningse Universiteit, 1614–1939*. Hilversum, Verloren.

ROEGIERS, J. and N.C.F. VAN SAS (2006). 'Revolution in the North and South, 1780–1830'. In J.C.H. Blom and E. Lamberts, eds. *History of the Low Countries*. New ed. Trans. J.C. Kennedy. New York: Berghahn.

ROELOFSEN, C.G. (2013). 'Röling, Bernardus Victor Aloysius (1906–1985)'. *BWN* 4.

ROOS, A.G. (1914). *Geschiedenis van de Bibliotheek Rijksuniversiteit Groningen*. Groningen: J.B. Wolters.

ROOY, P. DE (2016). 'Fortuijn, Wilhelmus Simon Petrus (1948–2002)'. *BWN* 6.

'Rosalind Franklin Fellowships'. RUG. <www.rug.nl/research/our-top-research>, accessed 10 Jun. 2018.

SAKHAROV, A. (2014). 'Andrei Sakharov: Biographical'. Nobel Media. <www.nobelprize.org/nobel_prizes/peace/laureates/1975/sakharov-bio.html>, accessed 21 Jul. 2018.

SANTESSON, M.C.G. et al. eds (1913). *Les Prix Nobel en 1913*. Stockholm: Imprimerie Royale.

SCOTT-SMITH, G. (2009). 'American Studies in the Netherlands'. In H. Krabbendam, C.A. van Minnen and G. Scott-Smith eds. *Four Centuries of Dutch-American Relations*. New York: SUNY Press.

SCYLLA, E.D. (2008). 'Bernoulli, Jakob (Jacob, Jacques, James) I'. *DSB* 19.

SHULTZ, W.W., P. VAN ANDEL, E. MOOYAART, and I. SABELIS (1999). 'Magnetic resonance imaging of male and female genitals during coitus and female sexual arousal'. *BMJ*, vol. 319: 1596–1600.

SHERRINGTON, C.S. and C. OVERY (2004). 'Langley, John Newport'. *ODNB*.

SJAAN&NOUT, dir. (2014). *For Infinity*. RUG. <www.youtube.com/watch?v=Beu0s3UpXll>.

SLUIS, R. TER (2009). 'Sieraad van de verlichting'. In Termeer and van Berkel eds.

SLUIS, J. VAN (2015). *De Academie van Vriesland: Geschiedenis van de Academie en het Athenaeum te Franeker, 1585–1843*. Gorredijk: Bornmeer.

SMIT, F. (2009). '1714 Geen Eeuwfeest'. In Termeer and van Berkel eds.

SMIT, F., ed. (2006). *Illustrious School: The Academy Building, the Historic Heart of Academic Groningen*. Groningen: Universiteitsmuseum.

SÖRLIN, SVERKER (2008). 'Arrhenius, Svante August'. *DSB* 19.

STEVENSON, D. (2004). *1914–1918: The History of the First World War*. London: Penguin.

Stichting Volkenkundige Collectie Nederland. SVCN. <www.svcn.nl>.

'Sustainable Society'. RUG. <www.rug.nl/research/sustainable-society>, accessed 13 Jul. 2018.

TAMMELING, B.P. (1978). *Honderd Vijfenzeventig Jaar AZG: Geschiedenis en Voorgeschiedenis van het Academisch Ziekenhuis Groningen*. Groningen: Academisch Ziekenhuis Groningen.

TERMEER, G. AND K. VAN BERKEL eds (2009). *Magazine 395: Grepen uit een Rijke Geschiedenis*. Groningen: RUG.

Think Bold: University of Groningen Strategic Plan, 2015–2020 (2015). Office of the University, RUG. <www.rug.nl/strategy>.

TOOMER, G.J. (1996). *Eastern Wisdom and Learning: The Study of Arabic in Seventeenth-Century England*. Oxford: Clarendon Press.

Universiteitsbibliotheek Groningen: Renovatie 2014–2017 (2017). Groningen: UB.

'Universities of Applied Science'. *Study in Holland*. <www.studyinholland.nl/education-system/dutch-institutions/universities-of-applied-sciences>, accessed 1 June 2018.

VANDERJACHT, A. (2004). 'Practicing Continuity: The Academy at Groningen, 1595–1625'. In A.A. MacDonald and A.H. Huussen, eds. *Scholarly Environments: Centres of Learning and Institutional Contexts, 1560–1960*. Leuven: Peeters.

VEEN, BEREND VAN DER (2013). *Wie was Jan Verleun?* Zutphen: Skipper Publishing (www.lulu.com).

VEN, J. VAN DER (2003). 'Groningse Loskoppen: Academierechtspraak in Groningen'. In A.H. Huussen Jr, ed. *Onderwijs en Onderzoek: Studie en Wetenschap aan de Academie van Groningen in de 17e en 18e Eeuw*. Hilversum: Verloren.

VENNING, T. (2004). 'Macdowell, William'. *ODNB*.

VERWEY, W.D. (1995). 'Bert V.A. Röling (1906–1985)'. In T.M.C. Asser Institute. *The Moulding of International Law: Ten Dutch Proponents*. The Hague: T.C.M. Asser Institute.

VISSER, E. (1964). *Universitas Groningana MCMXIV–MCMLXIV. Gedenkboek ter Gelegenheid van het 350-jarig Bestaan der Rijks-universiteit te Groningen Uitgegeven in Opdracht van de Academische Senaat*. Groningen: J.B. Wolters, 1964.

VRIES, N.W. DE, dir. (2011). *University of Groningen Lipdub: Mr Blue Sky*. RUG. <www.youtube.com/watch?v=oKE8O3xrK2I>.

WERFF, E.O. VAN DER (2003). *Martini Kerk en Toren*. Assen: Bureau Walburg, 2003.

WIELINGA, M. (2014). *Het Engelse Kamp, Groningen 1914–1918: De geschiedenis van 1500 Engelse militairen tijdens de Eerste Wereldoorlog*. Bedum: Profiel.

WILDE, I. DE (1979). *Aletta Jacobs in Groningen*. Groningen: RUG.

WILDE, I. DE (1987). *249 Vrouwen na Aletta Jacobs: Vrouwelijke Gepromoveerden aan de Rijksuniversiteit Groningen, 1879–1987*. Groningen: RUG.

WILDE, I. DE (1998). *Nieuwe Deelgenoten in de Wetenschap: Vrouwelijke Studenten en Docenten aan de Rijksuniversiteit Groningen, 1871–1919*. Assen: Van Gorcum.

WILDE, I. DE (2016). 'Klooster, Jantina Henderika van'. *Digitaal Vrouwenlexicon van Nederland*. Huygens Ing. <http://resources.huygens.knaw.nl/vrouwenlexicon/lemmata/data/klooster>.

WRIGHT, D.F. (2004). 'Renwick, James [alias James Bruce]'. *ODNB*.

'Yantai in 13 Steps: End of the Chinese Dream' (2018). *UK*, 30 Jan.

ZANDVOORT, R.W. (1941–63) 'Collegedictaten, 1941–1963'. UB, HS Add. 298.

Zeijlmaker, A. 'De beoefening der natuurwetenschappen'. In J. Kingma, W.R.H. Koops and F.R.H. Smit, eds. *Universitair Leven in Groningen 1614–1989*. Groningen: UB.

ZINKSTOK, E. and D. ROMASHUK (2011). 'Studenten pezen harder door BSA'. *UK*, 3 Feb.: 4–5.

INDEX

Z

V

W

Hero Jan Kars (1912)

Printed in Great Britain
by Amazon

63435393R00096